THE HARKLEAN VERSION

OF

THE EPISTLE TO THE HEBREWS

CHAP. XI. 28—XIII. 25.

Printed on the occasion of the Eighth International Congress of Orientalists held at Stockholm and Christiania, Sept. 1889.

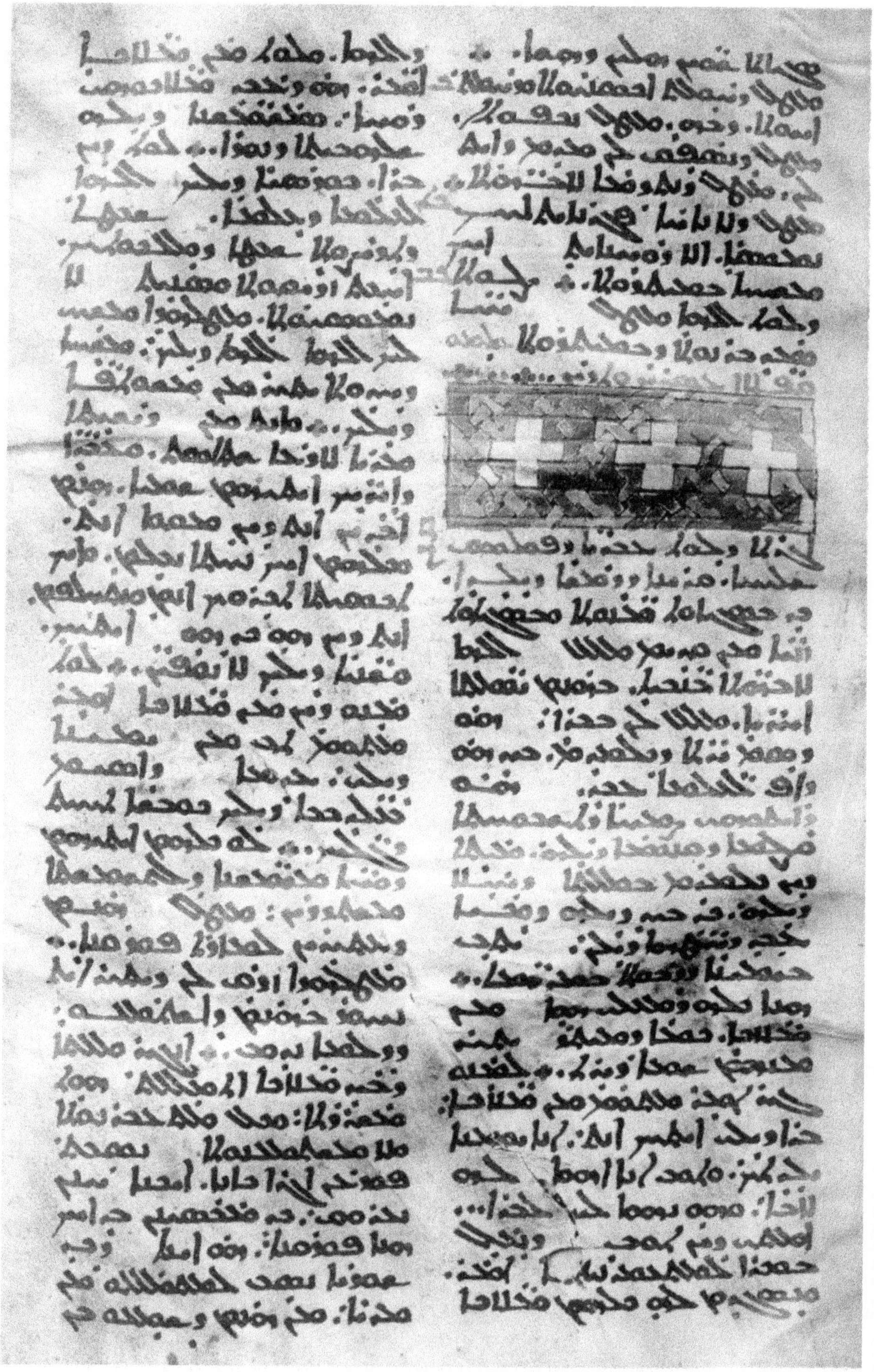

To face Title-page.

Cambridge University Press.

THE HARKLEAN VERSION

OF

THE EPISTLE TO THE HEBREWS

CHAP. XI. 28—XIII. 25.

NOW EDITED FOR THE FIRST TIME WITH INTRODUCTION
AND NOTES ON THIS VERSION OF THE EPISTLE.

BY

ROBERT L. BENSLY,

SENIOR FELLOW OF GONVILLE AND CAIUS COLLEGE AND LORD ALMONER'S
PROFESSOR OF ARABIC IN THE UNIVERSITY OF CAMBRIDGE.

CAMBRIDGE:
AT THE UNIVERSITY PRESS.
1889

CAMBRIDGE
UNIVERSITY PRESS

University Printing House, Cambridge CB2 8BS, United Kingdom

Published in the United States of America by Cambridge University Press, New York

Cambridge University Press is part of the University of Cambridge.

It furthers the University's mission by disseminating knowledge in the pursuit of education, learning and research at the highest international levels of excellence.

www.cambridge.org
Information on this title: www.cambridge.org/9781107623835

© Cambridge University Press 1889

First published 1889
First paperback edition 2014

A catalogue record for this publication is available from the British Library

ISBN 978-1-107-62383-5 Paperback

INDEX.

ERRATA.

In Chap. XII. 26, *for* ܗܪܝ *read* ܗܝܪ.

Page 8, line 6, *for* 'Diatesseron' *read* 'Diatessaron'.

„ 25, „ 8, *for* 'and τοιοῦτος' *read* 'and τοσοῦτος'.

In chap. xii. 13 for ܐܪܝܠܝܐ read ܐܪܝܠܐ.

A division should be marked between lines 21 and 22 of p. ܟ.

INTRODUCTION.

IN editing the latter portion of the Ḥarklean or so-called Philoxenian version[a] Prof. White had to rely solely on the Ridley MS. (No. 333, Library of New College, Oxford), which breaks off at the end of verse 27 of the eleventh chap. of the Epistle to the Hebrews. In spite of the large additions which have since been made to the stock of Syriac MSS. in European Libraries, this MS. remained the only authority (if we except certain Lectionaries not yet accurately examined) for the Epistles of St Paul (including the Epistle to the Hebrews)[b]. In 1876, however, the University Library of Cambridge purchased at the sale of the books of the late Jules Mohl a complete copy of the Ḥarklean version[c], from which I now publish the concluding chapters of the Epistle to the Hebrews. This MS., now classed as Add. 1700, is in oriental binding of red leather and consists of 216 parchment leaves, 9½ inches by 6½, with two columns of 37 to 40 lines on each page. The text is clearly written but without vowels, asterisks, obeli or marginal readings. At the beginning of the volume there are three tables of lessons, one for each of the three Classes under which the books are grouped, viz. :

---

[a] Actuum Apostolorum et Epistolarum tam Catholicarum quam Paulinarum versio Syriaca Philoxeniana ex Codice MS. Ridleiano in Bibl. Coll. Nov. Oxon. reposito nunc primum edita cum interpretatione et annotationibus Josephi White, S.T.P. Ling. Arab. apud Oxonienses Prof. Tom. I. Actus Apost. et Epist. Cath. Oxonii 1799, Tom. II. Epist. Paul. Oxonii 1803.

[b] The existence of MSS. where the Ḥkl. version of the Gospels is followed by the Pesh. of the other books (as in MS. 334, New Coll. Oxford, and Add. 17,124 Brit. Mus.) seems to indicate that there was, even in early times, a difficulty in procuring copies of the Ḥkl. version of the latter portion of the N. T.

[c] No. 1796, Catalogue de la Bibliothèque Orientale de feu M. J. Mohl, Paris, 1876.

I. The Gospels with the customary subscription, giving the date of their translation in the days of Philoxenus, A.D. 508, and of their recension based on three MSS. (as in the case of the Cod. Angelicus, Vat. 271 and 272, and Add. MS. 1903, Univ. Libr. Cambr.[a]) by Thomas of Harkel at the Enaton of Alexandria A.D. 616. This division concludes with a Diatesseron of the Passion of our Lord[b].

II. The Acts of the Apostles with the seven Cath. Epistles and a subscription similar to that printed by White. Then follows the unique copy of a Syriac translation of the two epistles of Clement of Rome, which was probably made in the school of Jacob of Edessa.

III. The Epistles of St Paul (ending with the Epistle to the Hebrews). Then follow, as here printed: (1) a subscription referring to an autograph of Pamphilus as the original textual authority for this division, and to two Gk. MSS. as the basis of the present revision; (2) the Colophon which states that the MS. was completed A. Gr. 1481 [A.D. 1170] in the little convent of Mar Saliba on the holy mountain of Edessa at the expense of Rabban Basil called Bar Michael of Edessa, so that he might have it for study and spiritual meditation and profit both of soul and body. The name of the scribe is Sahda of Edessa.

[a] A copy made by H. Petermann from a MS. dated A. Gr. 1521 (A.D. 1210), who states in his 'Reisen im Orient' (1860), vol. I. p. 127, that the Matrân of the Jacobites in union with the Church of Rome at Damascus lent him this MS. to make a copy, not being allowed to sell it, because a similar MS., about a century earlier, described (in vol. II. p. 12) as containing the New Test. in the Hkl. version, had disappeared during the persecution of the Christians at Aleppo, in 1850, having been either burnt or sold to an Englishman. If we consider the great rarity of MSS. of the Hkl. version containing more than the four Gospels, it seems not improbable that this Aleppo MS. is identical with that which forms the basis of the present publication. This presumption is strengthened by comparing the dates of the two MSS. A.D. 1170 and A.D. 1210. How Professor Mohl became possessed of our MS. is not known, but a suggestion has been made that it was presented to him by a traveller.

[b] Beginning thus: 'But when it was evening (Matt. xxvi. 20) he sat down and the twelve Apostles with him (Luke xxii. 14), and as they were eating' etc. (Matt. xxvi. 21). It differs from that contained in Add. MS. 1903, Univ. Libr. Cambr., which begins with 'Now the feast of unleavened bread drew nigh' etc. (Luke xxii. 1–7).

It is interesting to record here an incident in the history of this MS. about a century after it was written: On fol. 11. r. there is a notice, partially obliterated, the substance of which is repeated on fol. 1. r., to the effect that this MS. after the capture of Cilicia by the Tatars (or Huns) came to Sebaste or Sebastia (Siwâs), the city of the Martyrs[a], where it was redeemed and set at liberty like a slave by Rabban Daniel bar Ḥannun who presented it to the Church of Mar Theodorus in that city A. Gr. 1595 (A.D. 1284)[b].

To give a certain completeness to my work I have printed the 'Υπόθεσις and the Κεφάλαια of Euthalius in Greek and Syriac together with the lessons as rubricated in the text.

I have also collated the Epistle as edited by White with the two existing MSS., and chap. viii. 3 to ix. 10 with a Lectionary in the Brit. Museum.

To this I have appended an extract from a Massoretic MS. of the Brit. Museum bearing on the Ḥḳl. of this Epistle.

The main object of my notes is to determine as accurately as possible the readings attested by this version.

---

[a] A view of the interior of the monastery of the 40 martyrs at Siwâs is given in *Travels and Researches in Asia Minor etc.*, by W. F. Ainsworth, vol. ii. p. 1.

See also: *Missionary Researches in Armenia*, by Eli Smith and H. G. O. Dwight, p. 45.—*Notes from Nineveh*, by J. P. Fletcher, vol. i. p. 103.—*The Nestorians and their rituals*, by G. P. Badger, vol. i. p. 29.—*Asia Minor*, by H. J. van Lennep, vol. ii. p. 57.

[b] In a later notice written over the foot of the obliterated col. (fol. 11. r.), Yuḥannan called also Stephanos of Beth Severina, bar Yeshua', bar Behnam claims to be possessor of this MS.

B.   *b*

COLLATION OF THE MSS.

OF

THE ḤARḲLEAN VERSION OF THE EPISTLE TO THE HEBREWS WITH WHITE'S EDITION.

C = Add. MS. 1700, University Library, Cambridge.

O = No. 333, Library of New College, Oxford.

L = Add. MS. 12,139, British Museum, London (for Chap. VIII. 3—IX. 10).

Wh. = The text as edited by Jos. White.

TITLE.

+ ܕܦܘܠܘܣ ܫܠܝܚܐ C.

CHAPTER I.

3. ܕܝܢ inserted above line O.

7. ܘܠܘܬ C Wh., ܘܠܘ O.

9. ܡܛܠܗܕܐ C Wh., ܡܛܠ O.

CHAPTER II.

1. ܕܢܬܦܪܐܢܬ C Wh., ܢܬܦܪܐܢܬ O.—ܬܛܠܠܡ ܢܘܦܩ. O marg. (given incorrectly by Wh. as ܬܛܠܠܢ).

2. ܘܠܐ ܡܫܬܡܥܢܘܬܐ O (παρακοή).

3. ܐܫܬܪܪ C Wh., ܐܫܬܪܪܘ O.

4. ܘܒܬܕܡܪ̈ܬܐ C, ܘܬܕܡܪ̈ܬܐ (ܒ added above line) O.

5. ܠܡܬܥܡܪܢܝܬܐ C, ܡܬܥܡܪܢܝܬܐ O.

7. ܘܒܐܝܩܪܐ O, ܘܐܝܩܪܐ C (cf. ver. 9).

9. ܕܐܠܗܐ O, ܕ inserted later in C.

10. ܘܒܐܝܕܝ̈ܗ O, ܘܒܝܕ̈ܗ C.

13. ܗܐ ܐܢܐ O, ܗܐ ܐܢܐ C.

15. ܕܫܒܝܡ : O, ܕܢܒܝܐܡ : C.

Chapter III.

4. ܐܢܫ O, ܐܢܫܐ C (as Pesh.).

8. ܕܡܫܝܚܐ ܒ̄ ܒ̄, A blank space at end of line is so filled up in O.

10. ܕܠܐ C Wh., om. O.

15. ܠܠܒܘ̈ܬܐ C cf. ver. 8, ܠܒܘ̈ܬܐ O.

16. ܐܢܫܝܢ ܓܝܪ ܕܟܕ... C (τίνες γαρ...), ܐܢܫܝܢ ܓܝܪ ܕܟܕ. (ܐܢܫ written above the 1st word) O.—ܐܠܐ ܟܠܗܘܢ C O.

Chapter IV.

2. ܒܕܒܪܐ C O.

3. ܬܪ̈ܥܝܬܗ C.

7. ܘܫܒܝܥܝܐ before ܒܝܘܡ O, om. C.

14. ܕܥܒܪ ܐܢܘܢ ܠܫܡܝܐ C, ܐܢܘܢ ܠܫܡܝ̈ܐ O.

Chapter V.

4. ܗܘ ܠܗ C Wh., ܗܘ O.

5. ܐܦ deleted before ܘܒܫܪܝܐ O.—ܢܬܕܠܦ (ܐ prefixed pr. m.) O, ܢܬܕܠܦ C.

8. ܒܪܐ ܐܝܬܘ̄ C, ܐܝܬܘܗܝ ܒܪܐ with signs of transposition O.

11. ܕܢ̈ܘܦܠܐ marg. νωθροι O (not νωφοι as Wh.).

12. ∴ ܕܬܬܠܡܕܘܢ O marg. (not ܕܬܬܠܡܕܘܢ as Wh.).—ܡܠܦܘܬܐ C, ܡܠܦ̈ܢܘܬܐ O.

14. ܕܡܫܡ̈ܠܝܐ C.

Chapter VI.

2. ܘܕܣܝܡܐ C Wh., ܘܣܝܡܐ O.

4. ܕܪܘܚܐ C, ܠܪܘܚܐ O.

7. ܕܐܬܐ C.

8. ܕܫܘܠܡܗ̇ C O.

11. ܡܬܐܡܢܝܢ O, ܡܬܐܡܢܢ C.

13. ܘܠܐ ܡܕܡ C, ܕܠܐ ܡܕܡ O (the ܕ seems to have been originally ܘ).

16. ܡܘ̈ܡܬܐ C.

19. ܐܢܩܘܪܐ C, Add. MSS. 7183, 12,178,* Bar Hebr.,† ܐܢܩܘܪ̈ܐ O.—ܕܓܙܐ C, Add. MS. 12,178, Bar Hebr., ܒܓܙܐ O.—ܘܡܫܪ̈ܪܐ O, ܡܫܪ̈ܪܐ C.

Chapter VII.

3. ܕܠܐ ܐܒܐ ܕܠܐ ܐܡܐ O (ἀπάτωρ, ἀμήτωρ).

12. ܐܢܘܡܐ C.

14. ܗ̇ܘ ܫܪܒܬܐ C, ܫܪܒܬܐ O Wh.

17. O on margin, late hand, (sic) מַלְכִּי יֶֽדֶק.

20. ܕܣܛܪ Wh., ܣܛܪ ܕܠܘ O C (οὐ χωρίς).—.ܡܘ̈ܡܬܐ ܗ̇ܢܘܢ ܓܝܪ ܗܘܘ ܒܠܥܕ ܡܘ̈ܡܬܐ ܐܝܬ̈. C.

22. ܕܝܬܩܐ C.

26. ܠܐ ܒܝܫܐ. ܠܐ ܡܛܘܫܐ. O (ἄκακος, ἀμίαντος).

27. ܐܢܘܡܐ C.—ܡܪܒ O margin.

28. ܡܫܡܠܝ C, om. O, [ܡܐܡ] Wh. incorrectly.

* See below, p. 17.

† Gregorii Abulfaragii Bar Ebhraya in Epistulas Paulinas Annotationes Syriace edidit Maximilianus Loehr. Gottingæ, 1889.

Chapter VIII.

1. ܩܐܦܠܘܢ C.

3. ܘܩܘܪ̈ܒܢܐ C (δῶρά τε), ܩܘܪ̈ܒܢܐ O L.

4. ܒܪ C O L, ܒܪ Wh.—ܗܘ̈ܐ ܟܗܢܐ (signa transp.) L.

5. ܐܚܘܐ L.

6. ܕܕܝܐܬܝܩܝܢ O L, ܕܕܝܬܝܩܐ C.—ܝܬܝܪ C L, ܝܬܝܪܐ O.—ܕܒܫܘ̈ܘܕܝܐ O L, ܕܒܫܘ̈ܕܝܐ C.

7. ܐܠܘ C O, ܘܐܠܘ L.

8. ܕܝܬܝܩܐ (bis) C, ܕܝܬܝܩܝܢ (1°) ܕܝܐܬܝܩܝܢ (2°) L.

9. ܒܐܝܕܝܐ ܕܠܗܘܢ O L, ܒܐܝ̈ܕܝܗܘܢ C, ܒܐܝܕ ܕܠܗܘܢ Wh.—ܒܕܝܬܝܩܐ C, ܒܕܝܬܝܩܝܢ L.

10. ܗܝ ܕܝܬܝܩܐ C, ܗܝ ܕܝܐܬܝܩܝܢ O L.
ܕܐܝܣܪܐܝܠ C L.—ܒܡܕ̈ܥܐ L.

11. ܢܠܦܘܢ L.—ܘܪܒ L.

Chapter IX.

1. ܗܝܕܝܢ. C O L (τό τε was read as τότε).

3. ܬܪܝܢܐ C L, ܬܪܝܢܐ ܬܪܝܢܐ O.—
ܩܘܕܫ̈ܐ ܕܩܘ̈ܕܫܐ C O, on margin : קֹדֶשׁ קָדָשִׁים O.

4. ܒܗ C O L, ܒܗ̇ Wh.—ܘܩܐܒܘܬܐ C L.—
ܕܕܝܐܬܝܩܝܢ O L, ܕܕܝܬܝܩܐ C.—
ܣܛܐܡܢܘܣ O L, Add. MSS. 7183, 12,178, ܣܛܡܢܘܣ C, ϲταμνοϲ on margin O L.—
ܘܦܠܐܩ̈ܣ C O, ܘܦܠ̈ܐܩܐܣ L.—
ܕܕܝܬܝܩܐ C, ܕܕܝܐܬܝܩܝܢ O L.

5. ܕܡܛܠܠܝܢ O L, ܡܛܠܠܝܢ C.—Om. ܟܠ L.—
ܗܫܐ ܐܝܬ C L, ܐܝܬ O.

10. Om. ܟܠ L.

12. ܩܘܕ̈ܫܐ ܀ O, ܩܘܕܫܐ ܀ C.

13. C, O.

15. C.— C.

16. O, C.—
 C O.

17. C, om. O.—
 C, O,
[Wh.— O, . O.

19. C, cf. Add. MSS. 7183, 12,178, apparently
altered to O.

20. C.— C O.

22. deleted) O.

23. O.— C O.

24. C, O.

26. O, C.— C.—
 C, O.

28. C O, Wh.

CHAPTER X.

1. O, O.

6. O.— C, O.

9. ' C O.

12. . C (with points marking the order
of the words as they stand in O).

14. C, O.

16. C.—
 O, . C.—
 C O.

19. O C, om. O.

22. O, C.

23. ܘܡܗܝܡܢ C.

25. ܡܦܣܝܢ C, .ܡܦ̇ܣܝܢ O.

27. ܕܣܒܠܐ O, ܘܣܝܠܐ C.

29. ܕܕܝܬܩܐ C.

34. ܩܢܝܢܐ margin *πραξιν* O (a mistake for *υπαρξιν*). See margin, Acts ii. 45.—

ܘܕܡܩܘܐ C, ܘܡܩ̇ܘܐ O.

35. ܠܐ O, ܘܠܐ C.

37. Om. ܩܠܝܠ C.

Chapter XI.

6. ܗܘ C.

7. ܥܬܝܕ C Wh., om. O.

8. ܗܘ ܕܥܬܝܕ C, om. O. ܗܘ ܕܥܬܝܕ Wh. incorrectly.

9. ܥܡܪ C O.

10. ܕܗܘ C, ܗܘ O.

11. ετεκεν ⁘ ܝܠܕܬ } ܦܫܝܩܐ ܗܘܐ εστηκν (sic) } O margin (the latter omitted by Wh.).

13. ܗܠܝܢ (ܟܠܗܘܢ) C, ܗܢܘܢ written below the line O.

15. ܠܗܘ C O (ܘ evanescent in O), ܠܗ Wh.

16. ܡܠܠ C, ܡܠܠ ܡܠܠ O.—

ܢܬܩܪܐ. ܛܝܒ ܓܝܪ ܠܗܘܢ ܡܕܝܢܬܐ. C,
ܢܬܩܪܐ.. ܛܝܒ ܓܝܪ ܡܕܝܢܬܐ ⁘ O.

20. עֵשָׂו O margin.

24. ܟܕ ܪܒܐ ܗܘܐ C, ܟܕ ܪܒܐ ܗܘܐ, margin ΜΕΓΑC

ΓΕΝΟΜΕΝΟΝ O.

25. ܕܡܚܒܠܐ C, ܕܡܚܒܠܐ O.

26. ܠܗ O, om. C.

ܫܡܗ̈ܐ ܘܩܪ̈ܝܬܐ*

ܕܐܓܪܬܐ ܗܝ ܕܠܘܬ

ܦܠܝܡܘܢ ܘܫܘܡܠܗ̇ ܕܗܝ

ܕܠܘܬ ܥܒܪ̈ܝܐ

Philem. 2 ܘܠܐܦܦܝܐ ܚܠܦ ܟܠܢܫ
Hebr. ii. 9

vi. 19 ܢܛܥܡ ܡܘܬܐ ⁘ ܗܘ

ܕܐܚܝܕܗܘ ܠܢ ܐܝܟ

ܐܓܘܪܐ ܕܢܦܫܐ

vii. 23 ܘܣܓܝ̈ܐܐ. ܡܛܠ ܕܒܡܘܬܐ

ܡܬܟܠܝܢ ܗܘܘ ܠܡܩܘܝܘ.

ix. 4 ܗܝ ܕܒܗ̇ ܩܣܛܐܡܢܘܣ

ix. 19 ܕܕܗܒܐ. ܘܠܗ ܠܟܬܒܐ

ܘܠܟܠܗ ܥܡܐ ܪܣܣ

xi. 37 ܒܙ ܐܡܪ. ܐܬܢܣܪܘ

ܒܟܪܘܬܐ. ܒܡܥܙ̈ܐ

* From Brit. Mus. Add. MS. 12,178, fol. 216, v. col. 1. Add. MS. 7183, fol. 101, v. col. 2, contains 8 of these passages in an abridged form (all exc. ii. 9 and vii. 23). The variants are xi. 37 ܐܬܢܣܪܘ, xii. 21 ܕܡܬܚܙܝܢܗ, xiii. 19 ܕܒܥܓܠ; The Commentary of Bar Hebræus contains ii. 9 (beginning with ܐܝܟܢܐ, as quoted also in the Com. of Bar Ṣalibi Bod. Or. 560), vi. 19, xi. 37, xii. 8 (omitting ܐܝܬܝܟܘܢ) and xii. 21 (with the Ethpa. form as in Add. MS. 7183).

xii. 8   ܪܚܡܐ. ܐܝܟ ܕܡܗ̇ܦܟܝܢ

         ܐܘܣܝܦܘ̣. ܘܠܐ ܚܛܐ.

xii. 21   ܘܐܝܡܐ ܕܒܫܠܝ̈ܐ ܐܝܘܪ

xiii. 5   ܠܐ ܕܐܬܚܠܡ̈ܝܢ. ܡܐ ܗ̇ܘ

         ܠܐܪ ܐܢܬ ܚܡܘܣ̈ܐ.

xiii. 19   ܐܪܚܐ ܕܐܚܝܠ̣ܝ ܐܪܕ̈ܘ̣ܐ ܐܪܚܐ

         ܠܗ̇ . ܐܝܟ ܚܣܕܡܐ

         ܐܘܣܚܬ ܩܕܝܬܐ

         ܕܐܒܠܘܣܝܘ ܫܠܝܚܐ.

NOTES ON THE ḤARKLEAN VERSION OF THE EPISTLE TO THE HEBREWS.

TITLE.

Tischendorf has 'syr^p ep. Pauli ad Hebr.' This ascription of the authorship to St Paul is merely taken from the Latin title in White's edition. It is not found in White's Syr. title, which is correctly printed from Cod. O, but it now appears in Cod. C.

CHAPTER I.

3. φέρων τε] ܡ݂ܢ ܕܐܝܬ. Examples of ܡܢ for τε (where δὲ is not recorded as a variant) are rare. Cf. Acts ix. 29; xv. 4; xxi. 30. ܕܐܝܬ marg. ܡܕܒܪ ܡܠܟܐ ܡܗܕܪ ܡ݂ܕܒܪ O. Cf. marg. διοικῶν, κυβερνῶν, οἰκονομῶν. Euth. var. lect. ed. Zacag.

δι' ἑαυτοῦ (αὐτοῦ)] ܒܩܢܘܡܗ ܒܝܕ. Cf. Nöld., Syr. Gram. p. 158. It is the usual form in the Ḥkl. In 2 Cor. i. 19 we have ܒܝܕ ܒܩܢܘܡܗ ܘܐܟܣܝܠܘܣ.

14. In the Ḥkl. σωτηρία = ܦܘܪܩܢܐ (exc. Jude 3), σωτήρ = ܦܪܘܩܐ always.

CHAPTER II.

1. δεῖ = ܘܠܐ always in Ḥkl. except Mat. xxvi. 35 and the parallel passage, Mark xiv. 31. Cf. marg. in Luke xxiv. 7. The equivalents in the Pesh. are generally ܘܠܐ and ܙܕܩ but in this epistle ܚܫܚ.

τοῖς ἀκουσθεῖσιν] ܒܗܠܝܢ ܕܐܫܬܡܥ, not, as White, 'ad ea quae audita sunt' but 'to those who have been heard'. ܢܦܠ ܢܬܬܘܝܟ O marg. Cf. Chrys. 'Μήποτε, φησὶ, παραρρυῶμεν,' τουτέστι, μήποτε ἀπολώμεθα, μὴ ἐκπέσωμεν.

2. Cod. O gives here and in Chap. VII. 3. 26 (cf. the various readings) instances of the accent called ܪܠܬܡܣܐ (from ὑφὲν, according to its correct etymology) or ܪܝܐܣܝ (from a fancied derivation of ὑφὲν from ὑφαίνω). *See* Phillips, A letter by Mar Jacob, Bishop of Edessa, &c., pp. 25, 55, 82, 83, 92. Baethgen, Syr. Gram. des Mar Elias von Tirhan, p. 53. Duval, Gram. Syr. p. 158.

3. ὅστις = 'ܐ ܪܐܝܪܐ ܐܚܐ generally in Ḥkl.; sometimes we find the curiously literal translation 'ܐ ܬܝܪܐ ܐܚܐ, e.g. Mat. xxi. 33; Mark viii. 34; Luke xiv. 27, xxiii. 19; Jac. ii. 10.

ὑπὸ τοῦ κ. ὑπὸ τῶν, Ḥkl., cf. Pesh. In the Syr. of the Ὑπόθεσις ὑπὸ τοῦ κ. διὰ τῶν.

ܐܬܝܕܝܪܐ O and Syr. of the Ὑπόθεσις. The erroneous pl. is probably a reminiscence of the Pesh., where there is a pl. subject.

4. ποικίλος = ܪܐܕܚܐܣ Ḥkl. always; = ܪܐܠܬܣ Pesh. (exc. 1 Pet. iv. 10).

8. 'τὰ πάντα: syr^utr. ante ὑποτάξαι pon.' Tisch. This is incorrect with regard to the Ḥkl. which observes the usual order.

10. ܐܚܠܐ.ܐ. The addition of this expression shows that the translator referred δι' ὅν to Christ.

CHAPTER III.

6. We may safely assign the reading ἐάνπερ (not ἐὰν) to the Ḥkl., although Tisch. and Treg. have not ventured to do so. For 'ܐ ܐܚܐ ܪ is never used in this version for the simple ἐάν, whereas it stands for ἐάνπερ in Hebr. vi. 3 and for εἴπερ in Rom. viii. 9, 17; 1 Cor. xv. 15; 2 Thess. i. 6; 1 Pet. ii. 3.

14. γεγόναμεν τοῦ Χριστοῦ, Ḥkl.

16. C supplies the correct reading ܝܐ (but not the missing negative). In consequence of this emendation ܐܝܠܐ = τίνες (not τινὲς as Wh. and Tisch.).

CHAPTER IV.

2. White's rendering of the Ḥkl. 'cum non admisti essent fidei qui audierant' adopted by Tisch. is erroneous. The Syriac is a literal translation of μὴ συγκεκραμένους τῇ πίστει τοῖς ἀκούσασιν.

3. ܐܚܕܬܘܝܐܕ with pl. points = καταβολή, here and chap. ix. 26; Mat. xiii. 35; Luke xi. 50; John xvii. 24, in Cod. C. Comp.

also White's ed. Mat. xxv. 34; John xvii. 24; Eph. i. 4. It is always marked as pl. in the Pesh. N. T. ed. Lee, also in the edition of Urm. 1846 and of N. York, 1886.

11. ܒܗ̇ ܕܒ ܒܗ̇ ܒ'. Similarly ܠ is repeated in this construction, but in the case of ܡܢ, it is ܕ which is prefixed to the noun in the Ḥḳl. (cf. Rom. ix. 21; Jac. iii. 10, 11).

ἀπιστίας, Vulg. Ḥḳl. (text), (omitted by Tisch. and Treg.).

12. μυελῶν + καὶ ὀστέων, Pesh. Ḥḳl. (omitted by Tisch. and Treg.).

13. ܡܕܡܘܬܗܘܢ O. The obelus seems out of place here and should probably be transferred to the preceding ܗܘܢ.

Chapter V.

2. μετριοπαθεῖν = ܠܡܣܝܒܪ ܡܚ̈ܫܢܘܬܐ. White's proposal to emend ܡܚ̈ܫܢܘܬܐ must be rejected. The language is evidently derived from the paraphrase in the Pesh. . . ܕܢܚܫ ܚܫܗܘܢ.

3. 'ὑπὲρ ἁμαρτιῶν...[Syr. Hcl.]' Treg. There can however be but little doubt, especially in view of the rendering of ὑπὲρ ἁμ. in ver. 1, that ܡܛܠ ܚܛܗ̈ܐ = περὶ ἁμ. For in the Ḥḳl. ὑπὲρ with gen. = ܚܠܦ always, and περὶ with gen. = ܡܛܠ with but few exceptions, as John xii. 6 and 1 Pet. v. 7 (in which places the translation is varied because ܡܛܠ precedes), Mark i. 44; Luke v. 14; 1 John iv. 10.

4. ἀλλὰ καλούμενος, Ḥḳl.

Chapter VI.

2. βαπτισμῶν τε διδαχῆς, Ḥḳl.

6. ܕܬܘܒ .. ܠܡܬܚܕܬܘ] Instances of this mixed construction are found in Clem. Epist. II. 17, ܕܐܦ ܠܗܘܢ ܕܡܫܠܡ ܠܡܗܦܟܘ ܬܘܒ ܠܬܝܒܘܬܐ, Ceriani, Mon. sacra et prof. II. 1, pp. 12, xvi., Nöld., Syr. Gr. p. 198.

7. If the points are correct, our translator has taken εὐλογίας for acc. pl. instead of gen. sing. Similarly in 2 Pet. ii. 14 ἁμαρτίας has been taken for a pl. in both versions.

9. ἀδελφοὶ = ܐܚ̈ܝܢ. The pronoun is often suffixed to vocatives in Syriac when it does not occur in the original. This fact has not

been sufficiently recognised by Editors. Dr Lee, for instance, has frequently in such cases printed ܡܝܢܪ̈ for ܡܝܢܪ̈ (cf. Acts i. 16, ii. 29, 37, vii. 2, xiii. 15, 26, etc.).

14. The fact that White renders ܐܪܠܪ ܪ by *certe* is not sufficient reason for claiming the support of the Hkl. for the reading ἦ μήν, as against εἰ μήν or εἰ μή. We have the same phrase in the Syr. Hex. for εἰ μήν (with variants) in Ezech. xxxiii. 27, and for ἦ μήν (with variants) in Num. xiv. 35 and Job i. 11.

16. 'Syr^{utr}. ἀντιλογ. αὐτ.' Tisch. We cannot, however, always determine the order in cases where ܠܐ is involved, cf. Tit. iii. 2, Hkl.

CHAPTER VII.

11. Τίς ἔτι χρεία] τίς [+ ἔτι margin] ἦν χρ. Hkl. No Greek authority is recorded for ἦν, cf. chap. ix. 2, 9 and Luke xxiv. 17. The verb ἐστὶ is regularly translated in the Hkl. by ܐܘܗ, its tenses being eked out by ܐܘܗ, ἐγένετο. E.g. ἐστὶ = ܐܘܗܐܣܘܝ, ἦν = ܐܘܗ ܐܘܗܐܣܘܝ, ᾖ = ܐܘܗܐܣܘܝ ܐܢܘܗܝ. Both ἔσται and γενήσεται = ܐܢܘܗܝ, and in the rendering of imperat. and inf. the two verbs also coincide.

17. Both Tisch. and Treg. add the Hkl. to the authorities for μαρτυρεῖται. This passive form however is always represented by a pass. in the Hkl. The text implied is μαρτυρεῖ ✳ αὐτῷ⁄ γάρ. For the asterisk we should probably substitute an obelus.

20. In this verse the negative must be restored to the first clause. For καθ' ὅσον, instead of 'ܕ ܐܡܟܐ, we have ܗܠܐܟ ܐܡܠܐ, the common translation of τοσοῦτο. Οἱ μὲν γ. χ. ὀρκωμοσίας, omitted by homoeot. in O, is now found in C. Εἰσὶν is detached from γεγονότες (as in ver. 23) and here translated as though it were ἦσαν. This last change however is probably not due to a various reading but to the fact that, when Jewish ceremonial is spoken of as still going on, our translator is accustomed to throw it back into the past. Cf. chap. ix. 6, 7, 13, 25, xiii. 11.

22. καὶ not expressed in Hkl.

26. Ἔπρεπεν = ܐܘܗ ܐܪܐ. In the Hkl. ܐܪܐ is always used in translating πρέπει, as ܐܪ is, with the exception of this verse, in the Pesh.

·Chapter VIII.

3. δῶρά τε Ḥḳl. (C).

Chapter IX.

1. In the phrase 'ᴐ ᴋᴀᴄᴐ ᴆᴗᴋ = εἶχεν, ᴋᴀᴄᴐ ᴆᴗᴋ is not affected by the gender or number of its subject. Cf. chap. x. 2, xii. 9 ; Mat. xix. 22; Mark iii. 10, iv. 5, xii. 44, etc. (Mat. xxi. 28 is an exception in ed. Wh. but not in Cod. C.)
'Τότε Arm.' Treg. ; add Ḥḳl.

2. Ḥḳl. literally = ἐν ᾗ ἦν ἡ λυχ.

4. ᴄᴀᴐ ᴆᴗᴋᴙ. The classical construction of the relative, a variation of the more usual form, ᴆᴗᴋᴙ ᴀᴄᴀᴐ ver. 2. In 1 Cor. viii. 6 both forms occur. See T. Skat Rördam, Libri Judicum et Ruth sec. vers. Syr. Hex., p. 31.

9. Ḥḳl. prob. καθ' ὅν referring to καιρὸν (but the reference to σκηνῆς is grammatically possible).

28. ᴋᴀᴐᴧᴗ C O. This correction does away with the form ᴋᴆᴠᴧᴗ (Wh.), a pl. which, according to grammarians, does not exist.

Chapter X.

1. αἷς C, om. O—αἰ οὐδ. δύνανται C O.

2. ἐπεὶ [οὐκ] ἂν ἐπαύσαντο = ᴀᴗᴗᴆᴆᴋ ᴗᴄᴐᴀᴆᴗᴋ ᴋᴧ ᴋᴀ. The difficulty of accounting for this translation may be measured by the fact that Tisch. cites the Ḥḳl. for the omission, and Treg. for the insertion of the negative. The former seems to me correct, since ᴋᴧ ᴋᴀ is the regular equivalent for ἐπεὶ = alioquin. There seems to be some corruption in the next word (possibly of a construction similar to that in Mat. xi. 23 Ḥḳl.).

7. ὁ Θεὸς at the end of the verse Ḥḳl.

12. οὗτος δὲ—ἐν δεξιᾷ Ḥḳl.

16. διάνοιαν according to both MSS. as in viii. 10.

Chapter XI.

11. Σάρρα + στεῖρα οὖσα Ḥḳl.

13. ᴀᴐᴄᴐᴗ may stand for either κομισάμενοι or λαβόντες but not for the third variant προσδεξάμενοι.

14. πατρίς = ܐܬܪ with a possessive pronoun; in one passage (Mark vi. 1) an etymological translation is attempted, ܐܬܪ ܕܒܝܬ ܐܒܘܗܝ.

15. ἐμνημόνευον Ḥkl.

19. The Ḥkl. has δύναται (ܡܨܐ), not δυνατός (ܡܨܝܐ ܗܘܬ) —καὶ before ἐν παρ. is not expressed.

20. πισ. περὶ τῶν μελ. Ḥkl.

26. The authority of the Ḥkl. should be transferred from τῶν Αἰγύπτου (Tisch. Treg.) to τῶν ἐν Αἰγύπτῳ.

---

29. διέβησαν + οἱ υἱοὶ Ἰσραήλ (cf. Ex. xiv. 22, 29)—διὰ ξηρᾶς γῆς—κατεπόθησαν Ḥkl.

31. ἡ ἐπιλεγομένη πόρνη Ḥkl., and so our MS. in the Epist. of Clem. Rom. § xii. supported by the Constantinople MS.

εἰρήνη = ܫܝܢܐ always in Ḥkl.; = ܫܠܡܐ generally in Pesh. (but translated ܫܝܢܐ in Pesh. of Mat. x. 34; Luc. xi. 21, xii. 51; Acts xii. 20, xxiv. 3; Eph. ii. 14, 15; Jac. iii. 18; cf. Acts vii. 26; Col. i. 20). ܫܠܡܐ is also the rendering in the four disputed Cath. Epistles now printed with the Pesh., and in the Fragments of Isaiah published by Ceriani from Add. MS. 17,106, Brit. Mus., and assigned by him to the Philox. version (Mon. sacra et prof. v. 1).

32. καὶ τί] καὶ is not expressed in Ḥkl. nor in Pesh.—γάρ με— Βαράκ τε (or καὶ Βαρ.) καὶ Σαμ. καὶ Ἰεφ. Δα. τε Ḥkl.

τῶν ἄλλων προφητῶν = ܢܒܝܐ ܐܚܪܢܐ Ḥkl. and so the Pesh. (cf. 1 Cor. xiv. 29, Pesh.). But elsewhere in the Ḥkl. οἱ λοιποί and not οἱ ἄλλοι (ܐܚܪܢܐ ܗܢܘܢ) is rendered by ܕ ܫܪܟܐ or ܗܠܝܢ ܕܫܪܟܐ (ܗܢܘܢ).

34. στόματα] ܦܘܡܐ is without the pl. points both in the Ḥkl. and Pesh., cf. aciem Vulg.

35. γυναῖκες Ḥkl.

ἐτυμπανίσθησαν] Translated by ܐܬܦܫܚܘ. Cf. τυμπανίζεται, πλήσσεται, ἐκδέρεται, ἰσχυρῶς τύπτεται, Hesychius; τυμπανίζεται, ξύλῳ πλήσσεται, ἐκδέρεται, καὶ κρέμαται, Suidas. These extracts throw some light on the Ḥkl. rendering.

37. ἐπειράσθησαν, ἐπρίσθησαν Ḥkl.

38. ܗܘܐ ܕܐܝܬ (Cod.), these words should be transposed.—

probably ἐν ἐρημίαις Ḥḳl. ('ܣ being repeated before each of the following nouns, as in the Pesh.).

39. ܡܠܘܗܝ (Cod.), we must read ܡܘܡܠ as in the Pesh.—τὴν ἐπαγγελίαν Ḥḳl.

40. περὶ ἡμῶν κρεῖττόν τι Ḥḳl.

CHAPTER XII.

1. τοσοῦτον. ܪܐܣ ܐܝܟ. It would have been a convenient practice to translate τοιοῦτος by ܪܐܣ ܐܝܟܐ and τοιοῦτος by ܡܠܬܐ ܪܐܣ, but there are several other instances of the correspondence which is found here (e.g. Mat. viii. 10, xv. 33; Joh. vi. 9, xii. 37; Acts v. 8; and also Apoc. xviii. 17).—τρέχωμεν Ḥḳl.

2. σταυρὸς = ܨܠܝܒܐ Ḥḳl. always; = ܙܩܝܦܐ Pesh. generally; but in this passage, in Mark x. 21 and Luke xiv. 27 the Pesh. has ܨܠܝܒܐ.

3. ̄εἰς αὐτὸν, (or ἑαυτòν) Ḥḳl.

7. εἰς παιδίαν ὑπομένετε (imperat.).
τίς γάρ ἐστιν Ḥḳl.

8. νόθοι = ܡܡܙܪܐ, Arab. اوشاجٌ. So Darius Nothus = ܕܪܝܘܫ ܡܡܙܪܐ, cf. Payne Smith, Thes. Syr.
νόθοι ἐστε καὶ οὐχ υἱοὶ Ḥḳl.

9. δὲ not added Ḥḳl.

11. πᾶσα δὲ Ḥḳl.
πρὸς μὲν τὸ παρόν. Translated freely by Ḥḳl. as if it were πρὸς μὲν τὸν καιρὸν τὸν παρόντα.

15. δι' αὐτῆς Ḥḳl.

18. ὄρει ψηλαφωμένῳ.
καὶ γνόφῳ καὶ σκότῳ, or ζόφῳ Ḥḳl. (The Pesh. seems to have the order of the LXX. in Ex. x. 22; Deut. iv. 11, v. 22 (hebr. 19), καὶ σκ. καὶ γν.).

θύελλῃ is rendered in Ḥḳl. by ܥܠܥܠܐ, which has the sense of the original word עֲרָפֶל Deut. v. 19, (in the Pesh. by ܥܪܦܠܐ, as in Bar-Hebr., ed. Urm. and N. York, not ܥܪܦܠܐ as Lee and earlier Editors).

B.   *d*

20. θιγγάνειν is here rendered by ܐܪܟ (the constant rendering of ἅπτεσθαι except in Mark iii. 10) and not by ܬܩܣܙ as in the two other instances of its occurrence.—λιθοβ. without addition Ḥḳl.

21. Μωσῆς γὰρ Ḥḳl.

22. καὶ πόλει Ḥḳl.

23. πανηγύρει is construed with the preceding words.—ἀπογεγρ. ἐν οὐρ. Ḥḳl.

24. παρὰ τὸ τοῦʾΑβ. Ḥḳl. as in Pesh.

25. παραιτ. τὸν ἐπὶ γῆς χρημ. Ḥḳl.

28. ἔχομεν—λατρεύομεν—αἰδοῦς καὶ εὐλαβείας Ḥḳl.

CHAPTER XIII.

4. Our translator has understood ἐν πᾶσιν in a neuter sense. πόρνους δὲ Ḥḳl.

6. καὶ οὐ φοβ. Ḥḳl.

9. παραφέρεσθε, v. l. περιφ. Ḥḳl. ܥܕܚܕܚ. There is a similar variation and Ḥḳl. rendering in Jude 12, where Treg. doubtfully assigns παραφ. to the Ḥḳl., but περιφ. is translated as here in the Ḥḳl. of Eph. iv. 14. Cf. also 2 Cor. iv. 10 and Mark vi. 55.

οἱ περιπατήσαντες Ḥḳl.

10. ἐξουσίαν Ḥḳl.

11. The verbs are rendered by past tenses, as in Pesh. See note on chap. vii. 20.—τὸ αἶμα περὶ ἁμ. Ḥḳl.

ܪܚܠܣ] It seems necessary to make the word plural. Cf. chap. x. 6, 8, 12, 18, 26. ܪܚܠܣ = a special sin. See 1 John v. 16, 17 Ḥḳl. ܪܚܠܣ = sin.

13. ἐξερχώμεθα Ḥḳl.

15. Δἰ αὐτοῦ οὖν Ḥḳl.

17. ὑπὲρ τῶν ψ. ὑ. ὡς λόγ. ἀποδ. Ḥḳl.

18. πεποίθαμεν…ἔχομεν ἐν πᾶσιν, καλ. Ḥḳl.

20. Ἰησοῦν Χριστὸν Ḥḳl.

21. ἐν παντὶ ἔργῳ εἰς—ποιῶν ἐν ὑμῖν (without αὐτῷ)—omit τῶν αἰώνων. Ḥḳl.

22. ἀνέχεσθε Ḥḳl.

23. ἡμῶν Ḥḳl.

25. Ἀμὴν Ḥḳl.

Subs. Finita est Epistula ad Hebræos quæ scripta est ex Italia per Timotheum.

* Ὑπόθεσις τῆς πρὸς Ἑβραίους ἐπιστολῆς Παύλου.

Ἡ δὲ πρὸς Ἑβραίους ἐπιστολὴ δοκεῖ μὲν οὐκ εἶναι Παύλου διά τε τὸν χαρακτῆρα, καὶ τὸ μὴ προγράφειν, ὡς ἐν ἁπάσαις ταῖς ἐπιστολαῖς, καὶ τὸ λέγειν, πῶς ἡμεῖς ἐκφευξόμεθα τηλικαύτης ἀμελήσαντες σωτηρίας, ἥτις ἀρχὴν λαβοῦσα λαλεῖσθαι διὰ[a] τοῦ Κυρίου, ὑπὸ τῶν ἀκουσάντων εἰς ἡμᾶς ἐβεβαιώθη, συνεπιμαρτυροῦντος τοῦ Θεοῦ σημείοις τε, καὶ τέρασι; τοῦ μὲν οὖν ἠλλάχθαι τὸν χαρακτῆρα τῆς ἐπιστολῆς φανερὰ ἡ αἰτία· πρὸς γὰρ Ἑβραίους τῇ σφῶν διαλέκτῳ γραφεῖσα, ὕστερον μεθερμηνευθῆναι λέγεται, ὡς μέν τινες[b] ὑπὸ Λουκᾶ, ὡς δὲ οἱ πολλοὶ[c] ὑπὸ Κλήμεντος, τούτου γὰρ[d] καὶ σώζει τὸν χαρακτῆρα. τοῦ δὲ μὴ προγράφειν τὴν ἐπιστολὴν[e], αἴτιον ἡ ἀκολουθία· Ἀπόστολος γὰρ ἐθνῶν ὑπῆρχεν ὁ Παῦλος, ἀλλ᾽ οὐχὶ Ἰουδαίων, ἐπεὶ δεξιὰς ἔδωκε τῷ Πέτρῳ, καὶ τοῖς Ἀποστόλοις κοινωνίας, ἵνα αὐτὸς μὲν σὺν Βαρνάβᾳ εἰς τὰ ἔθνη, οἱ δὲ περὶ τὸν Πέτρον εἰς τὴν περιτομήν· ἐπειδὴ δὲ κοινωνία τὸ κήρυγμα, καὶ κατηχηθέντες ὑπῆρχον οἱ ἐξ Ἰουδαίων, ὡς ἀποστασίαν διδάσκει Παῦλος, εἰκότως τοῦ γνωρίσαι χάριν τὴν συμφωνίαν, Ἑβραίοις ἐπιστέλλει· γράφοντα δὲ πρὸς τούτους, προγράφειν Ἀπόστολον οὐ θέμις. μαρτυρεῖται δὲ καὶ ἐν τοῖς ἑξῆς ἡ ἐπιστολὴ ὑπάρχουσα Παύλου, τῷ γράφειν, ὅτι καὶ τοῖς δεσμοῖς μου συνεπαθήσατε. καὶ ἐκ τοῦ λέγειν, περισσότερον εὔχεσθε, ἵνα τάχιον ἀποκατασταθῶ ὑμῖν. καὶ[f] ἐκ τοῦ λέγειν, γιγνώσκετε τὸν ἀδελφὸν ἡμῶν Τιμόθεον ἀπολελυμένον, μεθ᾽ οὗ, ἐὰν τάχιον ἔρχηται, ὄψομαι ὑμᾶς. οὐδεὶς γὰρ ἄν, οἶμαι, ἀπέλυσεν εἰς διακονίαν Τιμόθεον, εἰ μὴ Παῦλος, καὶ τοῦτον τάχιον προσδοκῶν, τὴν ἰδίαν αὐτοῖς, ὡς ἔθος πολλαχοῦ, σὺν αὐτῷ παρουσίαν ἐπαγγέλλεται. πολλὰ δὲ καὶ ἄλλα γνωρίζουσιν ἡμῖν αὐτοῦ τυγχάνειν τὴν ἐπιστολήν, ὡς καὶ ἡ ἀνάγνωσις αὐτὴ προϊοῦσα διδάξει.

* Laur. Alex. Zacagnius, Collectanea Monumentorum Veterum Ecclesiæ Græcæ ac Latinæ, Vol. i., p. 669.

Tit. om. Παύλου Syr.

[a] περὶ τοῦ K. διὰ τῶν Zac., διὰ τοῦ K. ὑπὸ τῶν Mill (Nov. Test. Gr.), Matthaei (D. Pauli Epist. ad Hebr. et Col.), ὑπὸ τοῦ K. διὰ τῶν Syr.

[b] +λέγουσιν Syr.

[c] οἱ λοιποὶ Syr.

[d] τοῦ γὰρ Zac., τούτου γὰρ Mill Mat. Syr.

[e] +τὸ ὄνομα Mill Mat. cf. Syr.

[f] om. καὶ ἐκ τοῦ λέγειν...ἐπαγγέλλεται Syr.

28

* Κεφάλαια τῆς πρὸς Ἑβραίους ἐπιστολῆς Παύλου κβ'.

I. Θεολογία Χριστοῦ ἐν δόξῃ Πατρὸς, καὶ ἐξουσίᾳ τῶν πάντων, μετὰ τῆς καθάρσεως τῶν ἐπὶ γῆς, ἀφ' ἧς ἀνέβη εἰς τὴν ἐπουράνιον δόξαν.

II. Ὅτι οὐ λειτουργικὴ ἡ δόξα Χριστοῦ, ἀλλὰ θεϊκὴ, καὶ ποιητικὴ, διὸ οὐκ ἐπὶ τοῦ παρόντος αἰῶνος, ἐν ᾧ οἱ λειτουργοὶ, ἀλλ' ἐπὶ τῆς μελλούσης οἰκουμένης.

III. Ὅτι ἐσαρκώθη κατὰ διάθεσιν, καὶ συμπάθειαν, καὶ οἰκειότητα, τὴν πρὸς ἡμᾶς, ἐπὶ σωτηρίᾳ ἀνθρώπων, τῇ ἐκ θανάτου, ἐπὶ τῆς πρὸς αὐτὸν οἰκειώσεως.

IV. Ὅτι οὐ πιστευτέον Χριστῷ, ὡς Μωϋσῇ ἐπίστευσαν· καθ' ὑπεροχὴν δὲ τὴν Θεοῦ πρὸς ἄνθρωπον.

(1) Ἐν ᾧ ὅτι φοβητέον τῶν πάλαι τὴν ἔκπτωσιν.

V. Προτροπὴ σπουδάσαι εἰς τὴν προδηλουμένην κατάπαυσιν.

VI. Τὸ φοβερὸν τῆς κρίσεως παρὰ τῷ λόγῳ, τῷ διὰ πάντων, καὶ τὸ χρηστὸν τῆς χάριτος τῆς ἱερατικῆς παρὰ τῷ ὁμοιοπαθήσαντι ἡμῖν ἀνθρωπίνως.

VII. Ἐπιτίμησις ὡς ἔτι δεομένοις εἰσαγωγῆς.

(1) Ἐν ᾧ προτροπὴ εἰς ἐπίδοσιν, ὡς οὐκ οὔσης ἀρχῆς δευτέρας.

(2) Παράκλησις σὺν ἐπαίνῳ.

VIII. Ὅτι βεβαία ἡ ἐπαγγελία τοῦ Θεοῦ, καὶ ταῦτα σὺν ὅρκῳ.

IX. Περὶ Μελχισεδὲκ, τοῦ εἰς Χριστὸν τύπου κατὰ τὸ ὄνομα, καὶ τὴν πόλιν, καὶ τὴν ζωὴν, καὶ τὴν ἱερωσύνην.

(1) Ἐν ᾧ ὅτι καὶ τοῦ Ἀβραὰμ προετιμήθη.

X. Ὅτι παύεται ἡ τοῦ Ἀαρὼν ἱερωσύνη, ἡ ἐπὶ γῆς οὖσα· ἵσταται δὲ ἡ οὐράνιος ἡ Χριστοῦ, ἐξ ἑτέρου γένους, οὐ κατὰ σάρκα, οὐδὲ διὰ νόμου σαρκίνου.

* L. A. Zacagnius, Collectanea Mon. Vet., Vol. i., p. 671.
Tit. om. Παύλου κβ' Syr.
III. ἐπὶ τῆς] διὰ τῆς Mill Mat. Cramer Catena, Syr.
IV. om. οὐ Mill Mat. Cram. Syr.
VII. εἰσαγωγῆς] + εἰς διδαχὰς Syr., τῆς στοιχειώδους εἰσαγωγῆς Cram.
   (1) ἐν ᾧ] καὶ Syr.
   (2) καὶ παράκ. Syr.
VIII. καὶ τοῦτο Syr.

XI. Ὑπεροχὴ τῆς δευτέρας διαθήκης παρὰ τὴν προτέραν ἐν ἱλασμῷ, καὶ ἁγιασμῷ.
XII. Περὶ τοῦ αἵματος Χριστοῦ, ἐν ᾧ ἡ νέα διαθήκη, ὅτι τοῦτο ἀληθὲς καθάρσιον εἰς αἰεὶ, οὐ τὰ ἐν αἵμασι ζῴων τοῖς πολλάκις προσαγομένοις.
XIII. Μαρτυρίαι περὶ τῆς μόνης καθάρσεως, καὶ προσαγωγῆς πρὸς Θεόν.
1. Ἐν αἷς προτροπὴ τῆς ἐν πίστει προόδου.
XIV. Προτροπὴ σπουδῆς κατὰ φόβον τῆς ἐγγιζούσης κρίσεως.
XV. Περὶ τοῦ καλὴν ἀρχὴν εἰς καλὸν τέλος προσαγαγεῖν.
XVI. Περὶ πίστεως, τῆς καὶ τοὺς παλαιοὺς δοξασάσης.
XVII. Περὶ ὑπομονῆς ἐν ἀκολουθήσει Χριστοῦ.
XVIII. Περὶ σωφροσύνης ἕως καιρὸς κατορθώσεως, μὴ ἀποτύχωμεν αὐτῆς, ὡς Ἠσαῦ, μὴ εὑρὼν τόπον μετανοίας.
XIX. Ὅτι φοβερώτερα τῶν ἐπὶ Μωϋσέως τὰ μέλλοντα, καὶ πλείονος ἄξια σπουδῆς τὰ νῦν.
XX. Περὶ φιλαδελφίας, καὶ φιλοξενίας.
1. Ἐν ᾧ περὶ σωφροσύνης.
2. Περὶ αὐταρκείας.
3. Περὶ μιμήσεως πατρῶν.
XXI. Περὶ τοῦ μὴ σωματικῶς ζῆν κατὰ νόμον, ἀλλὰ πνευματικῶς κατὰ Χριστὸν ἐν ἀρετῇ.
XXII. Εὐχὴ πρὸς Θεὸν περὶ τῆς εἰς ἀρετὴν ἀγωγῆς, καὶ οἰκονομίας. Στίχοι οβ'.

XIII. — ἐν αἷς / καὶ Syr. (O).
XVII. ἐν ἀκολ. Syr. marg. (O). Syr. text in puritate.
XX. περὶ φιλοξ. καὶ φιλαδ. Syr.
XXII. περὶ * τῆς ζωῆς καὶ / τῆς εἰς Syr. (O). om. καὶ οἰκονομίας Syr.

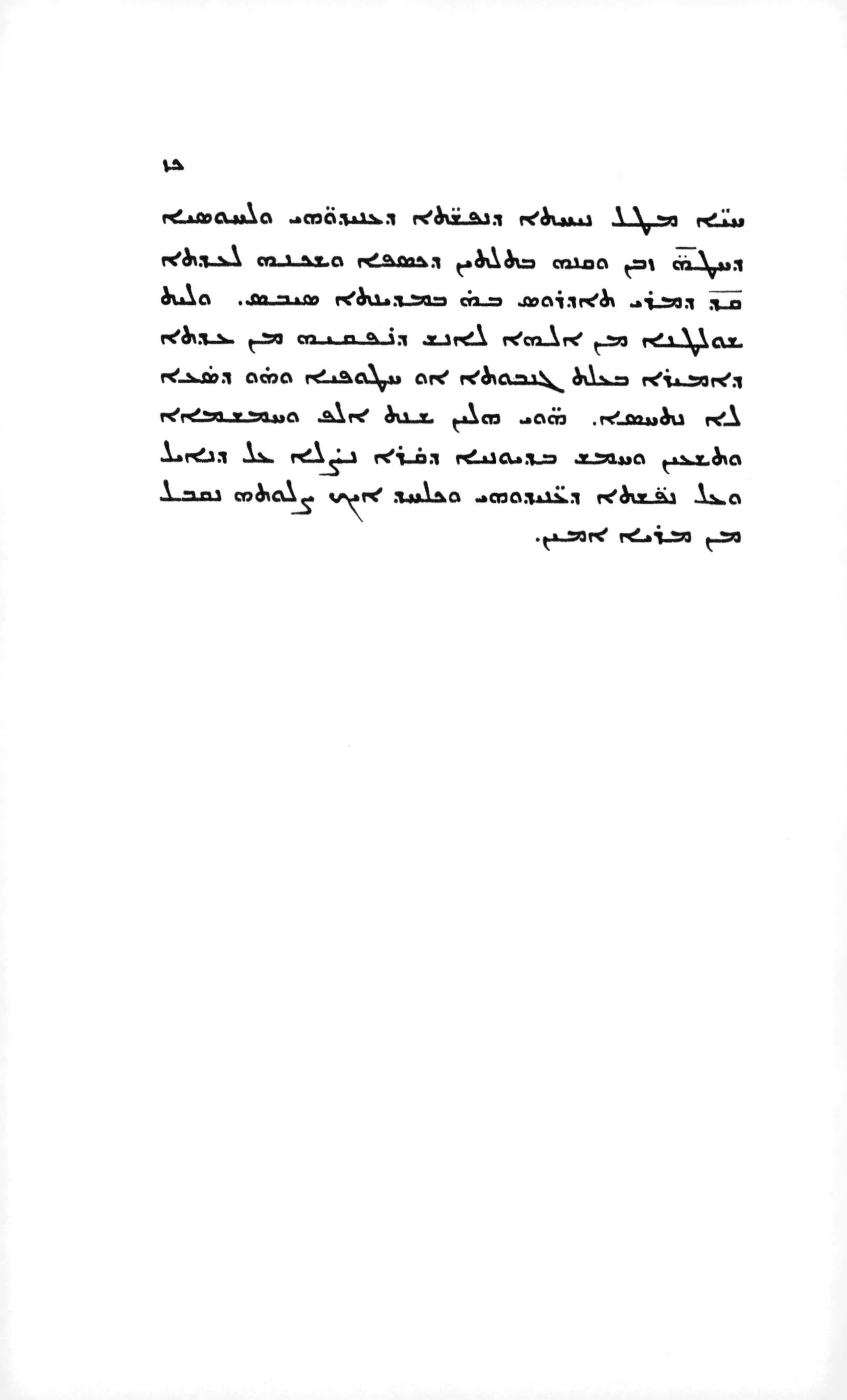

* Cod. C. f. 11. r. † Cod. C. f. 1. r.

HEBR. XI. 23.

HEBR. XI. 32.

HEBR. XII. 4.

HEBR. XII. 12.

HEBR. XII. 28.

HEBR. XIII. 10.

HEBR. XIII. 17.

[1] ܕܐܪܝܒܪܐ ܕܟܘܩܐ ܕܢܣܐ ܡܠܕ ܕܩܘܣܐ T.
[2] ܡܪܝܐ ܕܬܠܬܐ ܣܘܗܝܘܣ ܘܠܐܬܠܐ ܘܦܠܝܟ T.

HEBR. IX. 24.

HEBR. X. 15.

HEBR. X. 26.

HEBR. X. 32.

HEBR. XI. 1.

HEBR. XI. 8.

[1] ܩܒܠܬܘܢ ܐܓܘܢܐ ܕܐܘܠܨܢܐ. T.

[2] ܐܬܩܪܝ ܒܗܝܡܢܘܬܐ T.

ــ

HEBR. IV. 14.

HEBR. V. 12.

HEBR. VII. 1.

HEBR. VII. 18.

HEBR. VIII. 1.

HEBR. IX. 11.

² \ .

HEBR. IX. 16.

¹ . T.
² T.

HEBR. I. 1.

HEBR. II. 5.

HEBR. II. 14.

HEBR. III. 7.

HEBR. IV. 11.

These titles of the Lessons are taken from the body of the text in the Cambridge MS. (C). Some various readings are found in the Table of Lessons for the Epistles of S. Paul (ܩܘܒܐܣ ܕܐܓܪ̈ܬܐ, which stands at the beginning of the same MS. These are denoted by T.

[1] ܕܥܠ ܡܪܝܪܘܬܐ T.

[2] ܕܥܠ ܡܪܝܪܘܬܐ ܕܡܪܝܪܘܬ ܠܒܐ ܕܐܝܟ. T.

ܟܐ ܡܛܠ ܕܠܐ ܢܐܚܐ ܦܓܪܢܐܝܬ ܐܝܟ
[xiii. 9] ܢܡܘܣܐ. ܐܠܐ ܪܘܚܢܐܝܬ ܐܝܟ

ܟܒ ܡܫܝܚܐ ܒܡܫܡܫܢܘܬܐ. ܀ ܠܘ̱ܬܐ[a]
[xiii. 20.] ܕܠܘܬ ܐܠܗܐ ܡܛܠ ܫ̈ܢܝܐ[b]

ܘܡܫܒܚܢܘܬܐ ܕܒܡܫܡܫܢܘܬܐ ܫܠܡܘ
ܩ̈ܠܐܐ ܒܥܢܝܢ ܘܬܪܝܢ. . ܀ . . . ܀ .

[a] ܡܛܠ ܠܘ̱ܬܐ O. [b] ܫ̈ܢܝܐ * ܘ \ ܡܫܒܚܢܘܬܐ O.

 [a]

[x. 23]
[x. 32]
 [b]

[XI. 1]
 [c]

[XII. 1]
 [d]

[XII. 12]
 [e]

[XII. 18]
C. f. 209. r. 1. [f]

[XIII.1]
[][g]
---

[a] marg. O.
[b] \ O.   [c] marg. O.
[d] marg. O.
[e] : O.   [f] O.
[g] O has

[a] :

       [VI. 13]

 [VII. 1]

[b] :

 [VII. 11]

 [VIII. 7]

[c]

 [IX. 11]

[d]

 [X. 5]

[e].

[a] : O.   [b] O, om. C.

[c] O.   [d] O.

[e] . \ O.

ܩ̈ܠܐ ܕܐܟܪ̈ܬܐ ܝܚ

ܐܠܗܘܬܐ ܘܟܝܢܘܬܐ. ܡܛܠ
ܗܘܐ ܠܗ[a] ܒܥܠܡܐ ܗܢܐ ܐܝܬܘܗܝ
ܐܝܟܐ ܕܐܝܬ ܡܫ̈ܡܫܢܐ. ܐܠܐ
ܒܡܬܡܒܪܢܘܬܐ ܕܒܪ̈ܝܬܐ. ⁘
ܓ ܡܛܠ ܕܐܬܓܫܡ[b] ܒܣܘܦܐ
[II. 9] ܘܒܡܫܘܬܦܘܬ ܚܫܐ
ܘܒܚܝܘܬܐ ܕܠܘܬܢ. ܐܝܟ
ܕܠܦܘܪܩܢܐ ܕܒܢ̈ܝܢܫܐ ܗܘ ܕܐܡ
ܡܘܬܐ: ܒܝܕ ܒܝܬܘܬܐ ܕܠܘܬܗ.
ܕ [ܐ] ⁘ ܡܛܠ ܕܙܕܩ. ܠܡܗܝܡܢܘ
[III. 1] ܠܡܥܝܫܐ. ܐܝܟ ܕܗܝܡܢܘ
ܠܡܥܕܐ. ܐܝܟ ܕܒܡܠܝܘܬܐ ܕܝܢ
[ܒ] ܕܐܠܗܐ ܠܘܬ ܒܢ̈ܝܢܫܐ. ܕܒܗ. ܕܗ̇ܠܐ[c]
ܠܦܓܥ ܡܢ ܡܦܘܠܬܐ
ܗ ܕܗ̇ܢܘܢ ܠܬ̈ܪܥܐ. ⁘ ܡܣܬܒܪܢܘܬܐ
[IV. 1] ܠܡܐܢܝܢ ܕܢܦܫܬܐ ܗ̇ܝ
ܘ ܕܡܕܒܪܢܐ ܡܬܕܒܪܐ. ⁘ ܕܚܠܬܐ
[IV. 11] ܕܕܝܢܐ ܠܘܬ ܡܠܬܐ ܗܘ ܕܒܝܕ
ܟܠ. ܘܒܡܫܡܫܢܘܬܐ ܕܦܘܪܥܢܘܬܐ C. f. 208. v. 2.
ܕܚܝܢܘܬܐ: [d]ܠܘܬ ܗܘ ܕܒܝܕ ܒܪܡܘܬܐ
ܙ ܕܐܦ ܐܢܫܐܝܬ. ⁘ ܒܐܬܐ ܐܝܟ ܕܠܗ̇ܢܘܢ
[V. 11] ܕܒܕܒܠ ܗܝܡܢ ܟܠ ܡܠܬܐ

[a] ܠܗ altered to ܠܐ O.

[b] ܒܣܘܦܐ ... ܘ \ ܒܡܫܘܬܦܘܬܐ * O.

[c] ܘܕܗ̇ܠܐ CO, originally ܘܗ̇ܠܐ in C.

[d] ܕܠܘܬ O.

ܠܐ ܡܓܫܫ ܗܘܐ. ܡܫܬܡܗܕܪܐ[a]
ܕܝܢ ܐܦ ܒܗܠܝܢ ܕܒܬܪ ܗܢܐ
ܐܓܪܬܐ ܕܦܐܘܠܘܣ ܐܡܬܝ̣.
ܒܗ̇ܝ ܕܟܬܒ̣ ܕܐܦ[b] ܒܐܣܘܪ̈ܐ
ܕܠܝ ܒܟܒܠܝ ܚܫܬܘܢ. ܘܗܟܢ ܗ̇ܘ
ܕܐܡܪ ܝܬܝܪܐܝܬ[c] ܨܠܘ: ܐܡܒܥܐ
ܕܒܥܓܠ ܐܬܦܢܐ ܠܘܬܟܘܢ܀
ܗܟܢ̈ܐܬܐ ܕܝܢ ܘܐܣܬܪܗܒܬܐ ܡܫ̈ܘܕܥܝܢ
ܠܝ ܕܕܠܗ ܐܡܬܝ̣ ܐܓܪܬܐ.
ܐܝܟ ܕܐܦ ܗ̣ܘ ܦܪܝܫܐ ܒܗ̇
ܡܬܦܪܫ ܡܠܦ

C. f. 208. v. 1. *[d]ܦ̈ܠܐܐ ܕܐܓܪܬܐ ܕܠܘܬ ܥܒܪ̈ܝܐ.

ܐ [I. 1] ܬܐܘܠܘܓܝܐ ܕܡܫܝܚܐ ܒܬܫܒܘ̄
ܕܐܒܐ ܘܒܫܘܠܛܢܐ ܕܥܠ ܟܠ.
ܟܡ ܕܘܒܪܐ ܕܗ̇ܘܝܘ ܕܥܠ
ܐܪ̈ܟܐ: ܡܢ ܗ̇ܘ ܕܫܠܡ
ܠܬܫܒܘܚܬܐ ܫ̈ܒܝܚܬܐ܀
ܒ [I. 5] ܡܛܠ ܕܠܗ ܡܫܒܚܢܘܬܐ ܗܘܝ
ܬܫܒܘܚܬܗ ܕܡܫܝܚܐ. ܐܠܐ

[a] MS. ܡܫܬܣܗܕܪܐ.

[b] Hebr. x. 34.

[c] Hebr. xiii. 19.

* University Library, Cambridge, Add. MS. 1700 (C), New College Oxford MS. No. 333 (O).

[d] ܦܣܩܐܠ̈ܗܐ O.

ܡ̈ܡܠܠܐ ܕܐܟܪܙܘܬܐ ܟܠܝܐ ܗܘ ܟܠܗ̇ܬܐ:
ܠܘܬ ܓܝܪ ܥܡ̈ܡܐ ܒܡ̈ܡܠܠܐ ܕܝܠܗܘܢ
ܐܬܟܬܒܬ܆ ܘܡܬܐܡܪܐ[a]
ܕܠܫܪܬܐ ܐܬܦܫܩܬ. ܐܝܟ ܕܡ
ܕܐܬܥܝܪ ܐܡܪܢ. ܡܢ ܠܥܠܐ. ܐܝܟ
ܕܡ ܗܠܝܢ ܕܥܒܪܢ ܡܢ ܩܕܡܝܗܘܢ܆
ܕܗܘܐ ܓܝܪ ܐܦ ܡܫܘܬܦ ܡ̈ܡܠܠܐ.
ܕܠܐ ܕܝܢ ܢܣܒ ܫܡܗ ܒܪܫܐ ܕܐܟܪܙܘܬܐ.
ܟܠܗ̇ܬܐ. ܐܝܬܝܗ̇ ܗ̇ܝ ܢܨܝܚܘܬܐ.
ܥܠܝܡܐ ܓܝܪ ܕܫ̈ܠܝܚܐ ܐܝܬܝܗܘܢ
ܗܘܐ ܦܐܘܠܘܣ. ܐܠܐ ܠܘ ܕܝܗ̈ܘܕܝܐ܆
ܡܛܠ [b]ܕܡ̈ܫܝܚܐ ܕܫܡܫܘܬܐ ܝܗܒ ܗܘ
ܠܦܓܪܗܘܢ ܘܠܥܠܝ̈ܡܐ܆ ܐܡܝܢܐ
ܕܗܘܐ ܬܡ ܥܡ ܒܢܝܢܐ ܒܥܡ̈ܡܐ܆
ܗܠܝܢ ܕܝܢ ܕܒܥܬ ܦܓܪܗܘܢ ܒܟܪܘܙܘܬܐ.
ܡܛܠ ܕܝܢ ܕܒܫܡܫܘܬܐ ܗܘܬ
ܒܪܘܚܘܬܐ܆ ܘܠܫܒܝܐ ܐܫܬܥܒܕ
ܗܘܐ ܠܫܘܠܛܢ ܕܡܢ ܝܗܘ̈ܕܝܐ: ܐܝܟ
ܗ̇ܘ ܕܡܬܪܣܝܢܘܬܐ ܕܟܠܗ.
ܦܐܘܠܘܣ܆ ܙܕܩܐܝܬ ܟܕ ܫܟܐ
ܕܢܘܕܥ ܡܛܠ ܫܠܡܘܬܐ ܕܝܠܗ
ܟܬܒ ܠܥܡ̈ܡܐ. ܟܕ ܕܝܢ ܟܬ̈ܒ
ܠܘܬܗܘܢ܆ ܝܗܘ̈ܕܝܐ ܢܦܩܘܢ ܥܠܝܡܐ

[a] ܐܝܟ deleted at the end of the line.

[b] Gal. ii. 9.

ܘܠܒ̈ܢܝܗܘܢ ܒܬܪܝܗܘܢ ܟ̈ܠܗܘܢ ܠܥܠܡܐ
ܐܡܝܢ ܘܐܡܝܢ. ܠܥܠܡܝܢ ܐܡܝܢ..

ܫܘܒܚܐ ܡܢ ܟܠ ܠܬܠܝܬܝܘܬܐ: ܐܒܐ
ܘܒܪܐ ܘܪܘܚ ܩܘܕܫܐ. ܬܠܝܬܝܘܬܐ
ܚܣܝܐ ܫܘܒܚ. ܚܠܦ ܚܛܗܐ
ܕܐܟܬܒ̇ܬ ܐܢܐ. ܀ ܕܠܟܪܝܗ ܐܢܐ..

*ܘܦܐܠܗ̈ܘܬܐ ܕܐܓܪܬܐ ܕܠܘܬ ܚܒܪ̈ܐ ܀

ܐܓܪܬܐ ܕܝܢ ܕܠܘܬ ܚܒܪ̈ܝ.
ܡܫܬܒܪܐ ܗܝ ܕܠܐ ܐܝܬܝܗ̇
ܕܦܐܘܠܘܣ. ܡܛܠ ܫܘܠܠܗ̇† ܕܡܥܓܠ.
ܘܡܛܠ ܕܠܐ ܣܡ ܒܪܫܗ̇ ܫܡܗ
ܕܠܗ ܐܝܟ ܕܒܟܠܗܝܢ ܐܓܪ̈ܬܐ.
ܘܒܗ̇ܝ ܕܐܡܪ: [a]ܐܝܟܢܐ ܚܢܢ
ܢܦܘܩ ܐܢ ܢܒܣܐ ܥܠ ܦܘܪܩܢܐ
ܕܐܝܟ ܗܢܐ: ܗܘ ܕܡܢ ܒܪܝܫ ܫܘܪܝܐ
ܠܡܬܡܠܠܘ ܡܢ ܡܪܢܐ: ܒܗ ܗܘܢ
ܕܫܡܥܘ ܡܢ ܐܫܬܪܪܘ: ܒܗ ܗܘܐ
ܒܗܘܢ ܐܠܗܐ. ܒܐܬܘܬܐ ܘܒܬܕܡܪܬܐ ܀
ܕܡܛܠ ܡܢܐ ܗܘܝܐ ܡܢܝܢ

* New College, Oxford, MS. No. 333.
† ܫܘܠܡܗ̇ on margin.
a Hebr. ii. 3.

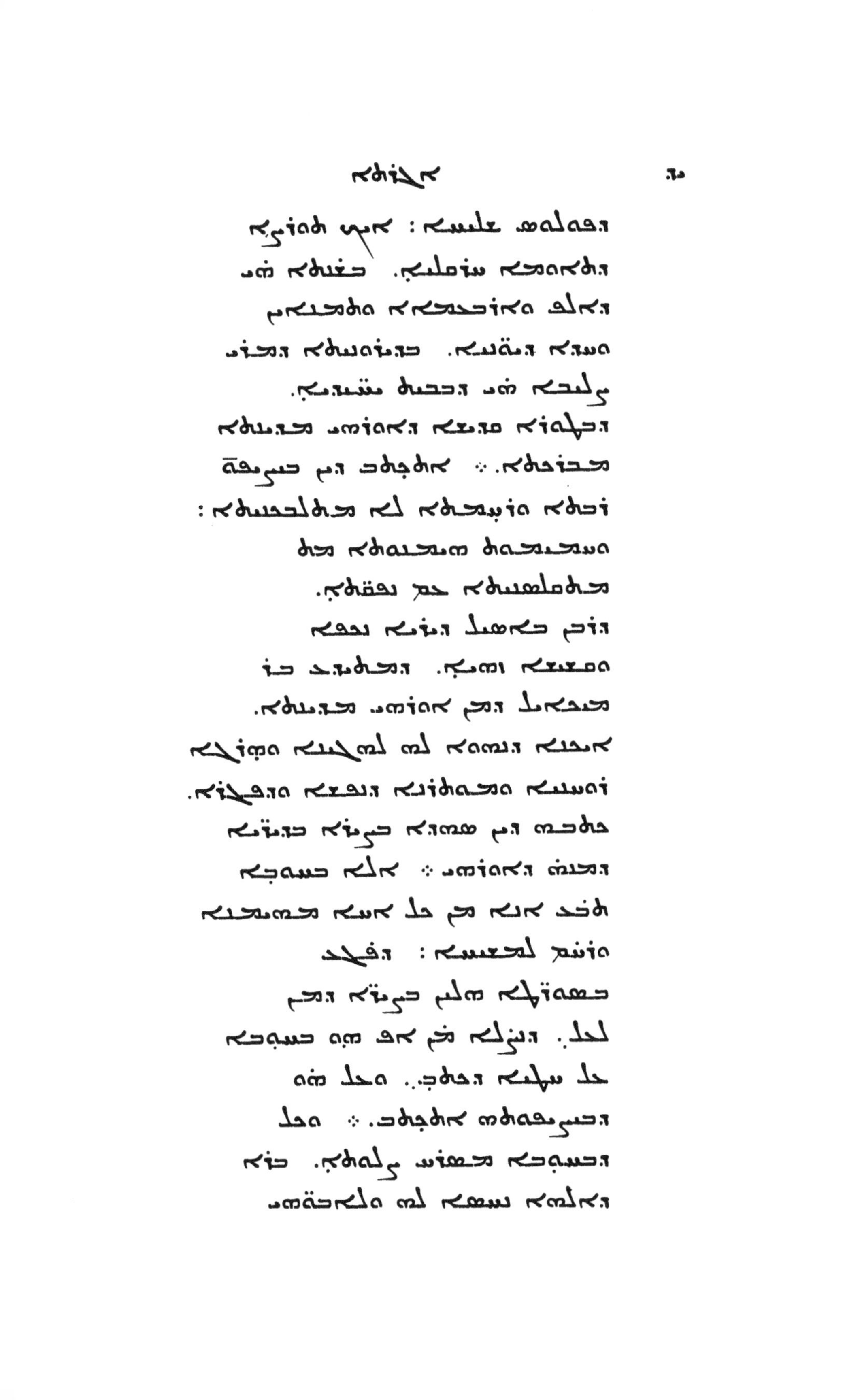

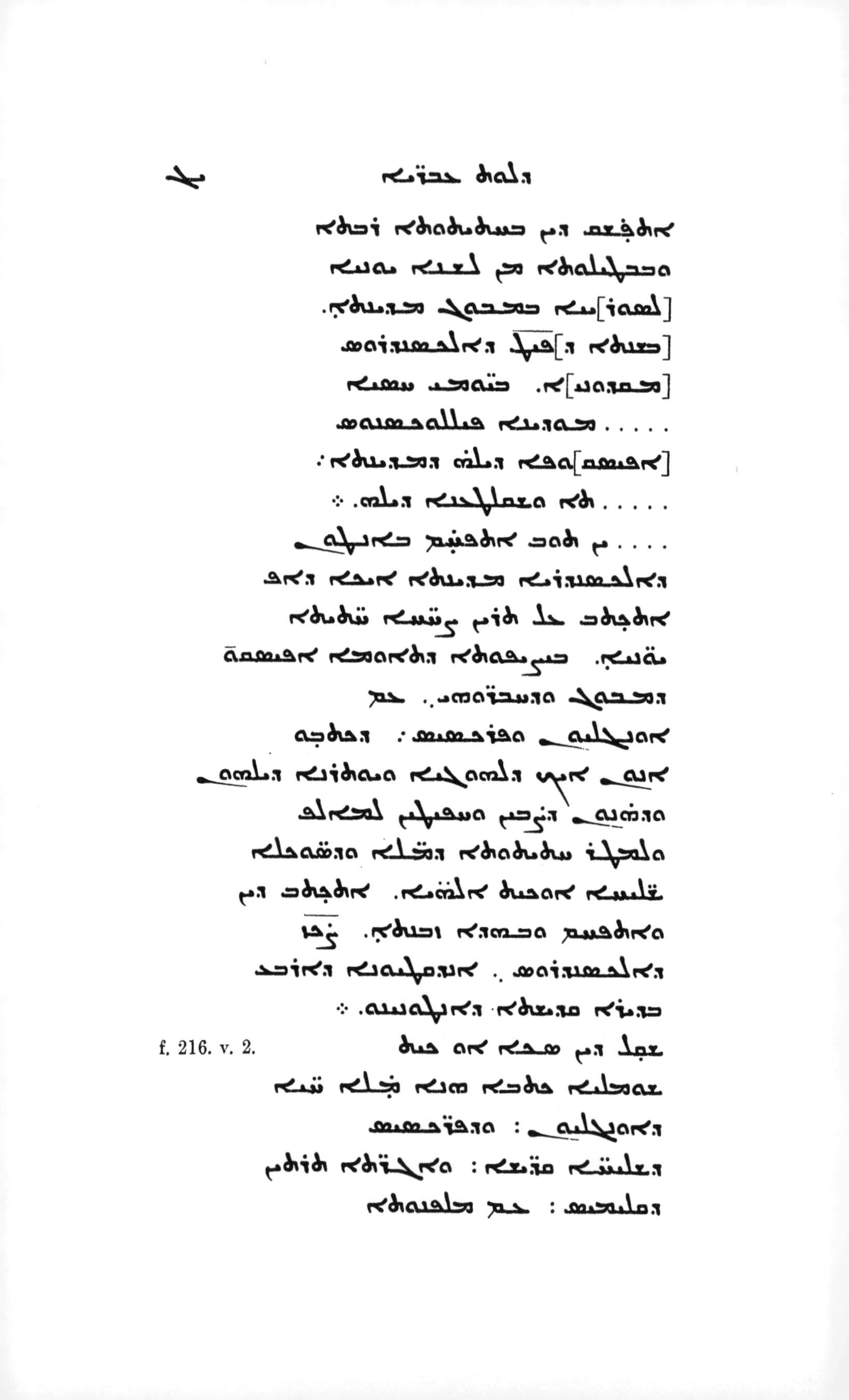

ܥܡ ܗܘ̇ ܕܐܢ ܒܥܓܠ ܢܐܬܐ ܚܙܐ ܐܢܐ
24 ܠܟܘܢ. ⁘ ܫܐܠܘ ܫܠܡܐ ܕܟܠܗܘܢ
ܕ̈ܒܪܢܐ ܕܟܠܟܘܢ ܘܕܟܠܗܘܢ ܩ̈ܕܝܫܐ ⁘
ܫܐܠܝܢ ܫܠܡܐ ܕܟܠܟܘܢ ܗܠܝܢ
25 ܕܡܢ ܐܝܛܠܝܐ. ⁘ ܛܝܒܘܬܐ ܥܡ
ܟܠܟܘܢ. ܐܡܝܢ. ܫܠܡܬ ܐܓܪܬܐ ܕܠܘܬ
ܥܒܪ̈ܝܐ ܕܐܬܟܬܒܬ ܡܢ ܐܝܛܠܝܐ
ܒܝܕ ܛܝܡܬܐܘܣ. ⁘ ܕܐܝܬ ܒܗ̇
f. 216. v. 1. ܩ̈ܪܝܢܐ ܬܠܬܐ. ܩ̈ܦܠܐܐ ܥܣܪܝܢ
ܘܬܪܝܢ. ܦܣ̈ܘܩܬܐ ܬܠܬܝܢ ܘܫܬܐ
ܦܬܓ̈ܡܐ ܫܒܥܡܐܐ ܘܬܠܬܐ.

ܐܬܚܬܡ ܟܬܒܐ ܗܢܐ ܕܦܘܠܘܣ
ܫܠܝܚܐ ܘܐܬܦܫܩ. ܡܢ ܝܘܢܝܐ
ܗܘ ܕܟܬܝܒ ܗܘܐ ܒܡܟܡܘܠ
ܡܕܝܢܬܐ: ܗܘ̇ ܕܐܝܟ ܗܘ̣ ܐܬܦܫܩ
ܗܘܐ ܡܢ ܝܘܢܝܐ ܕܐܝܬ [ܘܗܝ] ܗܘܐ
ܒܩܣܪܝܐ ܡܕܝܢܬܐ ܕܩܦܛܘܩܝܐ:
ܒܝܬ ܟܬ̈ܒܐ ܕܩܕܝܫܐ ܦܡܦܝܠܘܣ:
ܕܟܬܝܒ ܗܘܐ ܒܟܬܝܒܬ ܐܝܕܗ. ⁘
ܕܗܦܟܐ ܐܓܪ̈ܬܐ ܐܪܒܥܣܪ. ܕܐܝܬ
ܒܟܠܗܝܢ ܐܟܚܕܐ. ܩ̈ܪܝܢܐ. ܠܐ.
ܩ̈ܦܠܐܐ ܡܢ. ܦܣ̈ܘܩܬܐ ܡܢ.
ܦܬ̈ܓܡܐ. ܐܪܒܥܐ ܐܠܦܝܢ ܝܠܘ

ܠܢ̈ܦܫܬܐ ܕܝܠܟܘܢ ܘܐܫܬܡܥܘ.
ܗܢܘܢ ܓܝܪ ܫܗܪܝܢ ܚܠܦ
ܢ̈ܦܫܬܐ ܕܝܠܟܘܢ. ܐܝܟܢ ܕܡܠܬܐ
ܢܬܠܘܢ. ܐܝܟܢܐ ܕܒܚܕܘܬܐ
ܗܕܐ ܢܥܒܕܘܢ. ܘܠܐ ܟܕ
ܡܬܬܢܚܝܢ. ܠܐ ܡܘܬܪܢܘܬܐ ܗܝ
18 ܓܝܪ ܠܟܘܢ ܗܕܐ. ܀ ܨܠܘ ܡܛܠܬܢ.
ܬܟܝܠܝܢ ܓܝܪ ܕܬܐܪܬܐ ܫܦܝܪܬܐ
ܐܝܬ ܠܢ ܒܟܠܡܕܡ. ܟܕ ܫܦܝܪܐܝܬ
19 ܨܒܝܢ ܠܡܬܗܦܟܘ. ܝܬܝܪܐܝܬ
ܕܝܢ ܡܦܝܣ ܐܢܐ ܕܗܕܐ
ܬܥܒܕܘܢ. ܐܝܟܢܐ ܕܒܥܓܠ ܐܬܦܢܐ ܡܕ ܟܕ
20 ܠܟܘܢ. ܀ ܗܘ ܕܝܢ ܐܠܗܐ ܕܫܠܡܐ:
ܗܘ ܕܐܣܩ ܡܢ ܫܝܘܠ ܠܪܥܝܐ
ܕܥܢ̈ܐ: ܠܗܘ ܪܒܐ: ܒܕܡܐ
ܕܕܝܬܩܐ ܕܠܥܠܡ: ܠܡܪܢ
21 ܕܝܠܢ ܝܫܘܥ ܡܫܝܚܐ. ܢܫ[ܡܠܐ ܠܟܘܢ]
ܒܟܠ ܥܒܕܐ ܠܡܥܒܕ [ܨܒܝܢܐ]
ܕܝܠܗ. ܟܕ ܥܒܕ ܒܟܘܢ [ܗܘ]
ܕܫܦܪܐ ܩܕܡܘܗܝ. [ܒܝܕ]
ܝܫܘܥ ܡܫܝܚܐ. ܗܘ [ܕܠܗ]
22 ܬܫܒܘܚܬܐ ܠܥܠܡܝܢ ܐܡܝܢ. [ܡܦܝܣ]
ܐܢܐ ܕܝܢ ܠܟܘܢ ܐܚ̈ܝ. ܐܬܛܝܒܘ
ܠܡܠܬܐ ܕܒܘܝܐܐ. ܐܦ ܓܝܪ ܒܥܕ
23 ܙܥܘܪ̈ܬܐ ܫܕܪܬ ܠܟܘܢ. ܀ ܕܥܘ
ܠܐܚܘܢ ܕܝܠܢ ܛܝܡܬܐܘܣ ܕܐܫܬܪܝ..

ܦܘܢܝ ܕܗܠܟܘ. ܦܫܝܩܐ ܕܬܫ̈ܒ
ܬ̈ܚܡܝ ܕܒܪܘܟܬܐ ܕܐܘܚܕܢܘܬܐ:
10 ܐܝܬ ܠܢ ܡܕܒܚܐ. ܕܡܢܗ
ܠܡܐܟܠ ܠܐ ܐܝܬ ܠܗܘܢ ܫܘܠܛܢܐ:
ܠܗܢܘܢ ܕܠܡܫܟܢܐ ܦܠܚܝܢ.
11 ܕܚܝ̈ܘܬܐ ܓܝܪ ܕܗ̇ܢܝܢ ܕܥܐܠ
ܗܘܐ ܕܡܐ ܡܛܠ ܚܛ̈ܗܐ ܠܒܝܬ
ܩܘܕ̈ܫܐ ܒܝܕ ܪܒ ܟܘܡܪ̈ܐ. ܕܗܠܝܢ.
ܦ̈ܓܪܐ ܢܘܩܕܝܢ ܗܘܘ ܠܒܪ ܡܢ
12 ܡܫܪܝܬܐ. ܡܛܠܗܕܐ ܐܦ ܝܫܘܥ.
ܐܝܟܢܐ ܕܢܩܕܫ ܒܝܕ ܕܡܐ ܕܝܠܗ
ܠܥܡܐ̇ ܠܒܪ ܡܢ ܬܪܥܐ ܚܫ.
13 ܢܦܘܩ ܗܟܝܠ ܠܘܬܗ ܠܒܪ ܡܢ
ܡܫܪܝܬܐ̇. ܟܕ ܚܣܕܐ ܕܝܠܗ
14 ܡܛܥܢܝܢ. ܠܐ ܓܝܪ ܐܝܬ ܠܢ ܗܪܟܐ
ܡܕܝܢܬܐ ܕܡܩܘܝܐ̇. ܐܠܐ ܠܗ̇ܝ
15 ܕܥܬܝܕܐ ܒܥܝܢ. ܀ ܒܝܕܗ ܗܟܝܠ
ܢܩܪܒ ܕܒܚܬܐ ܕܬܫܒ̄ܘ ܒܟܠܙܒܢ
f. 216. r. 2. ܠܐܠܗܐ. ܗܢܘ ܕܝܢ ܦܐܪ̈ܐ ܕܣ̈ܦܘܬܐ
ܕܡܘܕܝܢ ܠܫܡܗ ܕܝܠܗ. ܀
16 ܠܛܝܒܘܬܐ ܕܝܢ ܘܠܫܘܬܦܘܬܐ̇ ܠܐ
ܬܛܥܘܢ. ܒܕܐܝܟ ܗܠܝܢ ܓܝܪ
ܕܒ̈ܚܐ ܡܫܬܦܪ ܐܠܗܐ ܦܫܝܩܐ
17 ܒܡܘܒܪܢܐ ܕܡܕܒܪ̈ܢܐ. ܐܬܛܦܝܣܘ

11. Cod. ܣܛܗܐ.

f. 216. r. 1.
9   ﻤ̄ﻗ / ﻝﻛ

25 ܚܙܘ ܠܐ ܬܫܬܐܠܘܢ ܡܢ ܗܘ
ܕܡܡܠܠ. ܐܝܟܢܐ ܗܢܘܢ ܠܐ ܚܪܘ:
ܕܐܫܬܐܠܘ ܡܢ ܗܘ ܕܡܡܠܠ
ܥܠ ܐܪܥܐ. ܗܟܢ ܡܬܦܪܐܬ ܚܢܢ.
ܗܢܘܢ ܕܡܢ ܗܢܐ ܕܡܢ ܫܡܝܐ
26 ܡܗܦܟܝܢ ܐܦܝܢ. ܕܗܘ ܕܩܠܗ
ܠܐܪܥܐ ܐܙܝܥ ܗܝܕܝܢ: ܗܫܐ ܕܝܢ
ܐܫܬܘܕܝ ܟܕ ܐܡܪ: ܬܘܒ ܚܕܐ
ܙܒܢ ܐܢܐ ܡܙܝܥ ܐܢܐ: ܠܘ ܒܠܚܘܕ
27 ܠܐܪܥܐ. ܐܠܐ ܐܦ ܠܫܡܝܐ. ܀ ܗܝ
ܕܝܢ ܕܬܘܒ ܚܕܐ ܙܒܢ. ܡܚܘܝܐ
ܠܫܘܚܠܦܐ ܕܗܠܝܢ ܕܡܙܕܥܙܥܝܢ
ܐܝܟ ܥܒ̈ܝܕܬܐ. ܐܝܟܢܐ ܕܢܩܘܘܢ ܗܠܝܢ
ܕܠܐ ܡܙܕܥܙܥܝܢ. ܩܢܝܢܐ ܒܕܘܟܝܐ
ܕܐ̈ܢܫܘܬܐ ܦܪ̈ܝܫܐ ܬܬܒܥܐ ܐܘܣ.
ܕܟܠܝܬܐ. ܘܕܡܟܐ ܘܫܡܥܝܢ
ܕܟܘܢܘܣܛܝܛܘܦܘܠܝܣ
ܐܬܝܒܢ ܘܒܐܦܝܣܘܣ. ܘܕܡܠܟܐ
ܘܣܛܝܛܘܣ ܘܟܠܗܘܢ ܡ̈ܠܟܐ
28 ܬܩܝܦܝ ܫܦܝܪܐ. ܡܛܠ ܗܢܐ ܟܕ
ܡܠܟܘܬܐ ܠܐ ܡܙܕܥܙܥܢܝܬܐ ܩܒܠܝܢ.
ܐܝܬ ܠܢ ܛܝܒܘܬܐ ܟܕ ܗܝ
ܕܦܠܚܝܢ ܐܝܟ ܕܫܦܪ ܠܐܠܗܐ. ܒܡ
29 ܒܢܟܦܘܬܐ ܘܒܕܚܠܬܐ. ܐܦ ܓܝܪ
ܐܠܗܐ ܕܝܠܢ. ܢܘܪܐ ܡܫܠܡܢܝܬܐ ܡܦ / ܕ
XIII. 1 ܗܘ. ܀ ܪ̈ܚܡܬܐ ܐܚܘܬܐ ܬܬܩܪܪ.

17 [ܒܒܘܟܪܘ]ܬܗ ܕܝܠܗ. ܝܕܥܝܢ ܐܢܬܘܢ
ܓܝܪ. ܕܐܦ ܡܢ ܒܬܪܟܢ ܟܕ
ܨܒܐ ܕܢܐܪܬ ܒܘܪܟܬܐ ܐܣܬܠܝ.
ܕܬܝܒܘܬܐ ܓܝܪ ܕܗܦܟܬܐ ܠܐ ܐܫܟܚ.. ܩܦ ܬܠ
18 ܘܟܕ ܬܘܒ ܡܢ ܕܫܒܩܐ ܒܟܢ.⁘ ܠܐ
ܓܝܪ ܐܬܩܪܒܬܘܢ ܠܛܘܪܐ ܡܬܓܫܫܢܐ.
ܘܠܢܘܪܐ ܕܝܩܕܐ. ܘܠܥܪܦܠܐ
19 ܘܠܚܫܘܟܐ ܘܠܥܠܥܠܐ. ܘܠܩܠܐ
ܕܫܝܦܘܪܐ ܘܠܩܠܐ ܕܡ̈ܠܐ: ܠܗܘ
ܕܗܢܘܢ ܕܫܡܥܘܗܝ ܐܫܬܐܠܘ
20 ܕܠܐ ܬܬܬܘܣܦ ܠܗܘܢ ܡܠܬܐ. ܠܐ
ܡܣܝܒܪܝܢ ܗܘܘ ܓܝܪ ܠܗܘ ܡܐ
ܕܐܬܦܩܕܘ. ܕܐܦܢ ܚܝܘܬ ܥܒܐ
21 ܬܓܫܦ ܒܛܘܪܐ ܬܬܪܓܡ. ܘܗܟܢܐ
f. 215. v. 2. ܕܚܝܠܐ ܐܝܬܘܗܝ ܗܘܐ ܗܘ ܡܐ
ܕܡܬܚܙܐ. ܡܘܫܐ ܓܝܪ ܐܡܪ.
22 ܕܕܚܝܠܐ ܐܢܐ ܘܪܬܝܬܐ. ܐܠܐ
ܐܬܩܪܒܬܘܢ ܠܛܘܪܐ ܕܨܗܝܘܢ.
ܘܠܡܕܝܢܬܐ ܕܐܠܗܐ ܚܝܐ ܐܘܪܫܠܡ
ܫܡܝܢܝܬܐ. ܘܠܪ̈ܒܘܬܐ ܕܚܝܠܐ
23 ܕܡ̈ܠܐܟܐ. ܘܠܥܕܬܐ ܕܒܘܟܪ̈ܐ ܕܟܬܝܒܝܢ
ܒܫܡܝܐ. ܘܠܐܠܗܐ ܕܝܢܐ ܕܟܠ
ܘܠܪܘܚܬܐ ܕܙܕ̈ܝܩܐ ܕܐܫܬܡܠܝܘ.
24 ܘܠܝܫܘܥ ܡܨܥܝܐ ܕܕܝܬܝܩܐ ܚܕܬܐ.
ܘܠܕܡܐ ܕܪܘܣܣܐ ܕܡܡܠܠ
ܛܒܬܐ ܝܬܝܪ ܡܢ ܗܘ ܕܗܒܝܠ.⁘

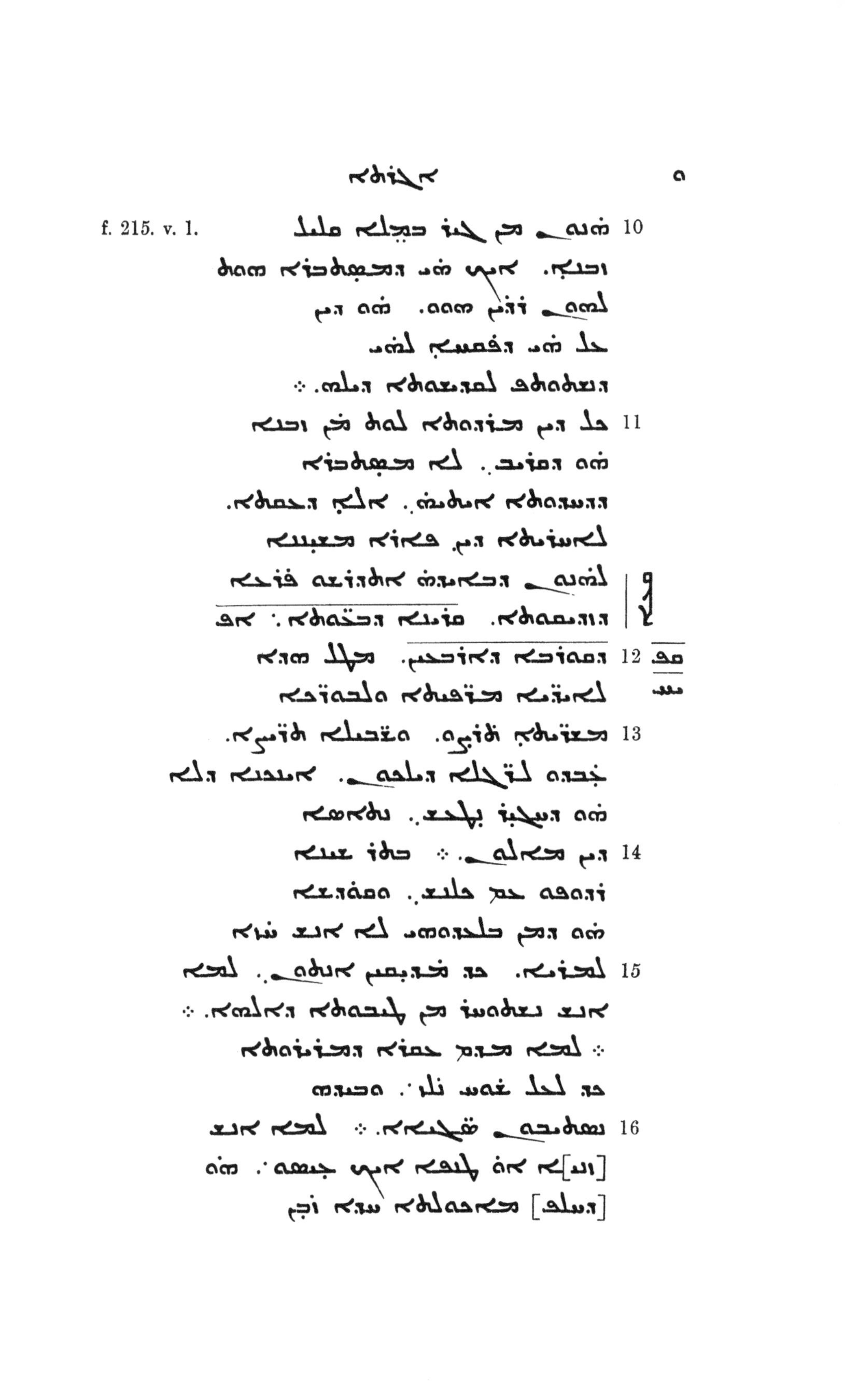

9

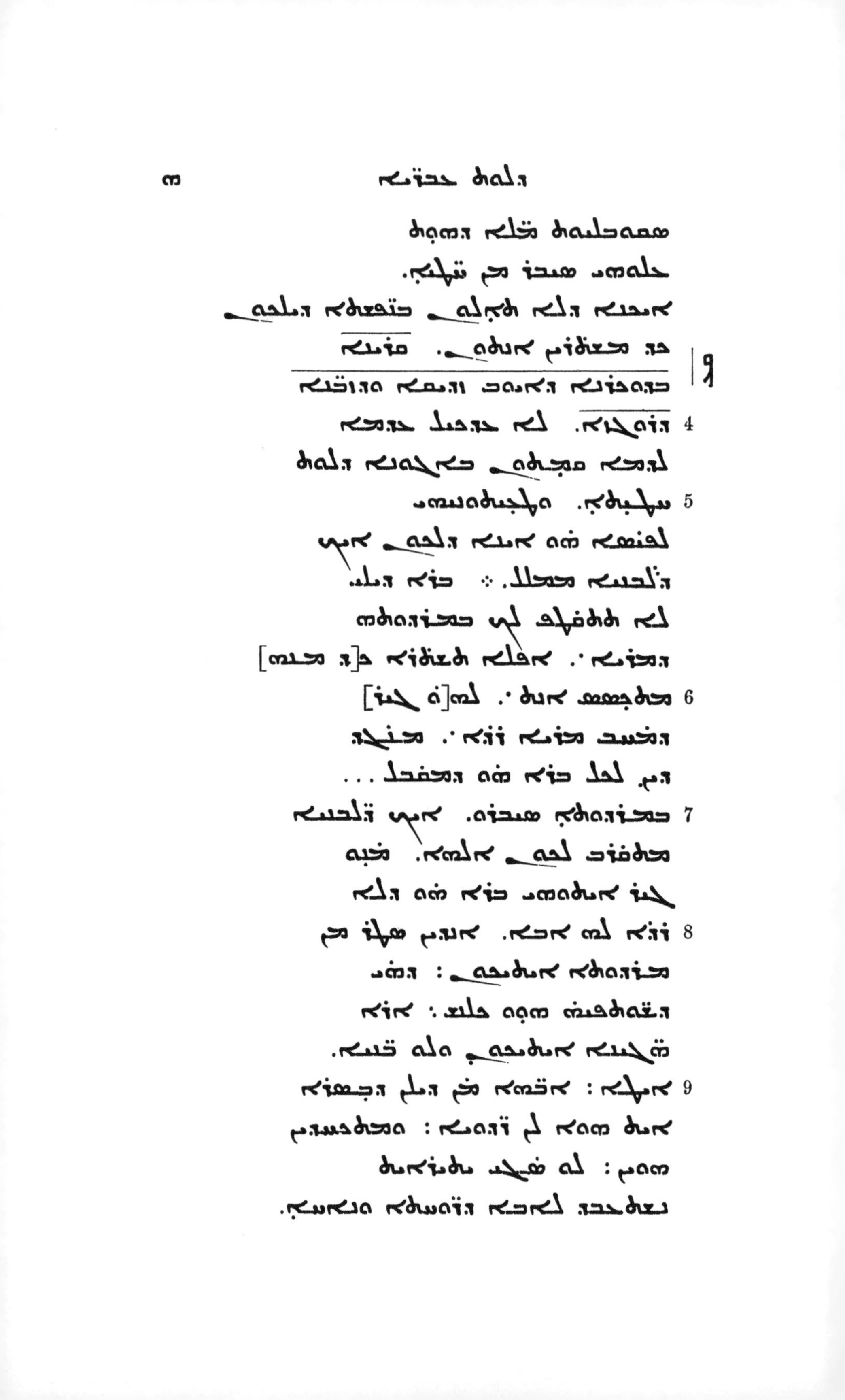

ܐܬܢܣܪܘ. ܒܩܛܠܐ ܕܣܝܦܐ
ܡܝܬܘ. ܐܬܟܪܟܘ ܒܦܪ̈ܘܬܐ. ܒܡܫ̈ܟܐ
ܕܥܙ̈ܐ. ܟܕ ܚܣܝܪܝܢ܆ ܐܠܝܨܝܢ܆
38 ܡܬܒܐܫܝܢ. ܠܗܘܢ ܕܠܐ ܐܫܬܘܝܘ
ܕܢܗܘܐ ܗܘܐ ܥܠܡܐ. ܟܕ ܒܚܘܪ̈ܒܐ
ܛܥܝܢ܆ ܘܒܛܘܪ̈ܐ ܘܒܡܥܪ̈ܐ
39 ܘܒܚ̈ܘܠܢܐ ܕܐܪܥܐ. ܀ ܘܗܠܝܢ
ܟܠܗܘܢ ܟܕ ܐܣܗܕܘ ܒܝܕ
ܗܝܡܢܘܬܐ. ܠܐ ܢܣܒܘ ܫܘܘܕܝܐ.
40 ܟܕ ܐܠܗܐ ܡܛܠܬܢ ܡܕܡ ܕܡܝܬܪ
ܩܕܡ ܚܙܐ܃ ܐܝܟܢܐ ܕܠܐ ܒܠܥܕܝܢ ܡܘ / ܝ
XII. 1. ܢܬܓܡܠܘܢ. ܀ ܒܪܡ ܗܟܝܠ ܐܦ
ܚܢܢ ܟܕ ܕܐܝܬ ܗܕܐ ܐܝܬ ܠܢ f. 215. r. 2.
ܕܣܚܪܐ ܠܢ ܥܢܢܐ ܕܣܗ̈ܕܐ܃
ܟܕ ܫܒܩܝܢ ܡܢܢ ܟܠ ܬܩܝܠܘܬܐ܃
ܐܦ ܠܚܛܝܬܐ ܕܥܝܩܐܝܬ
ܚܕܪܐ ܠܢ. ܒܝܕ ܡܣܝܒܪܢܘܬܐ
ܢܪܗܛܝܘܗܝ ܠܐܓܘܢܐ ܗܢܐ
2 ܕܩܕܝܡ ܣܝܡ ܠܢ. ܟܕ ܚܝܪܝܢ
ܒܗܘ ܪܫܐ ܘܡܫܡܠܝܢܐ
ܕܗܝܡܢܘܬܐ ܝܫܘܥ. ܀ ܗܘ
ܕܚܠܦ ܚܕܘܬܐ ܕܣܝܡܐ
ܗܘܬ ܠܗ ܣܝܒܪ ܨܠܝܒܐ܆
ܟܕ ܥܠ ܒܗܬܬܐ ܒܣܪ܆ ܘܒܝܡܝܢܐ
ܕܟܘܪܣܝܐ ܕܐܠܗܐ ܝܬܒ. ܀ ܀
3 ܐܬܚܫܒܘ ܓܝܪ ܠܗܘ ܕܕܐܝܟܢ ܗܕܐ

31 ܠܐܦ̈ܝ ܫܒܥܐ ܝܘ̈ܡܝܢ. ܒܗܝܡܢܘ̄
ܪܚܒ ܗ̇ܝ ܕܡܬܐܡܪܐ ܙܢܝܬܐ:
ܠܐ ܐܒ݂ܕܬ݂ ܥܡ ܗ̇ܢܘܢ ܕܠܐ
ܐܬܛܦܝܣܘ: ܕܩܒܠܬ݂ ܠܓܫ̈ܘܫܐ
ܥܡ ܫܠܡܐ. ܦܪܝܫܐ ܒܕܘܒܪܝܐ
32 ܕܦ̈ܘܩܕܐ. ܡܢܐ ܬܘܒ ܐܡܪ ܐܢܐ.
ܚܘܦܐ ܓܝܪ ܠܝ ܙܒܢܐ ܕܐ
ܡܫܬܥܝܐ ܐܢܐ: ܥܠ ܓܕܥܘܢ:
ܘܒܪܩ: ܘܫܡܫܘܢ: ܘܝܦܬܚ:
ܘܕܘܝܕ ܘܫܡܘܐܝܠ: ܘܫܪܟܐ
33 ܕܢܒܝ̈ܐ: ܗܠܝܢ ܕܒܝܕ ܗܝܡܢܘܬܐ
ܙܟܘ ܒܐܟ̈ܘܢܐ ܠܡܠܟܘ̈ܬܐ: ܦܠܚܘ
ܙܕܝܩܘܬܐ: ܩܒܠܘ ܫܘܘܕ̈ܝܐ: ::
34 ܥܒܪܘ ܒܩܘ̈ܡܬܐ ܕܐܪ̈ܝܘܬܐ: ܕܥܟܘ
ܚܝܠܐ ܕܢܘܪܐ: ܥܪܩܘ ܡܢ
ܦܘܡܐ ܕܣܝܦܐ: ܐܬܚܝܠܘ ܡܢ
ܡܚܝܠܘܬܐ: ܗܘܘ ܚܝ̈ܠܬܢܐ ܒܩܪܒܐ:
35 ܝܗܒܘ ܡܥܪ̈ܬܐ ܕܢܘܚܪ̈ܝܐ: ܢܦ̈ܩܝܢ
ܢܫ̈ܐ ܡܢ ܡܝܬܘܬܐ ܚܝ̈ܬܐ ܕܠܗܝܢ.
ܐܚܪ̈ܢܐ ܕܝܢ ܐܬܢܓܕܘ ܟܕ ܠܐ ܩܒܠܘ
ܦܘܪܩܢܐ. ܐܝܟܢܐ ܕܠܩܝܡܬܐ
36 ܡܫܬܪܬܐ ܢܣܒܘܢ. :: ܐܚܪ̈ܢܐ ܕܝܢ
ܕܒ̈ܙܚܐ ܘܢܓ̈ܕܐ ܢܣܝܘܢܐ ܢܣܒܘ ::
ܬܘܒ ܕܝܢ ܕܐܣܘܪ̈ܐ ܘܕܒܝܬ
37 ܢܛܘܪܬܐ. ܐܬܪܓܡܘ. ܐܬܢܣܝܘ.

34. Cod. ܚܝܠܬܢܐ.

ܐܓܪܬܐ ܕܠܘܬ ܥܒܪܝܐ

ܕܦܘܠܘܣ ܫܠܝܚܐ.

*   *   *   *   *

*   *   *   *   *

ܒܗܝܡܢܘܬܐ   *   *   *   xi. 28
ܥܒܕ ܠܦܨܚܐ ܘܠܐܫܝܕܘܬ ܕܡܐ ·
ܐܝܟܢܐ ܕܠܐ ܗܘ ܕܡܚܒܠ ܗܘܐ
ܒܒܘܟܪܐ ܢܩܘܫ ܒܗܘܢ ܀ ܀
29 ܒܗܝܡܢܘܬܐ ܥܒܪܘ ܝ̈ܡܐ
ܕܐܣܘܦܐܠ ܠܝܒܫܐ ܫܘܡܫܐ
ܐܝܟ ܕܒܝܕ ܐܪܥܐ ܡܢܬܫܬܐ : ܕܗܘ
f. 215. r. 1. ܕܒܗ ܢܣܝܢܐ ܢܦܩܘ ܡܨܪ̈ܝܐ
30 ܐܬܒܠܒܘ. ܀ ܒܗܝܡܢܘܬܐ ܫܘ̈ܪܝܗ
ܕܐܝܪܝܚܘ ܢܦܠܘ · ܟܕ ܐܬܦܪܟܘ

Cambridge University Library, Add. MS. 1700, fol. 214. vers. col. 2.

ܐܝܓܪܬܐ ܕܝܠܗ ܕܡܪܝ

ܕܩܘܠܘܣ ܫܠܝܚܐ